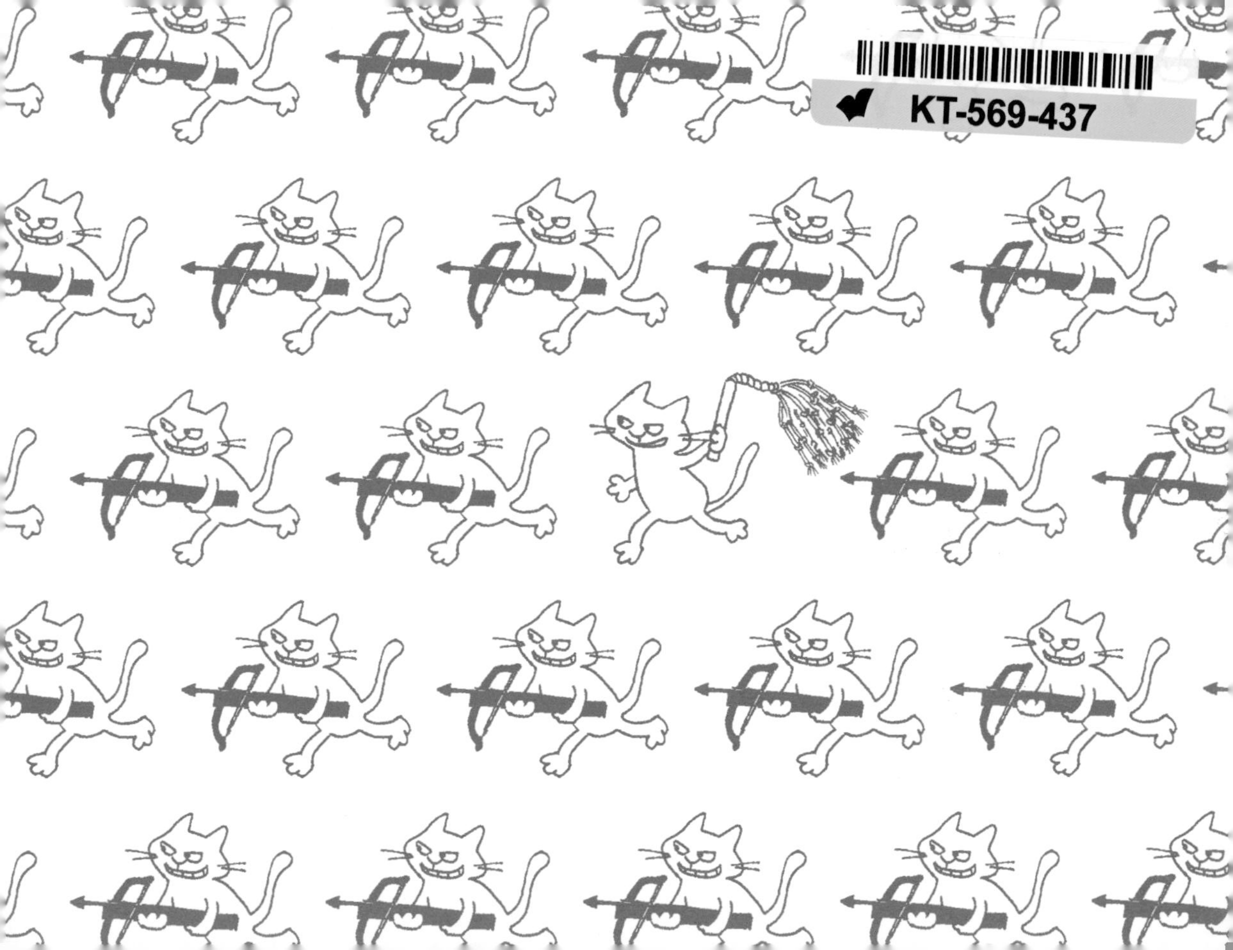

EVIL CATS

When Fluffy Cats Get Mean

by elia anie

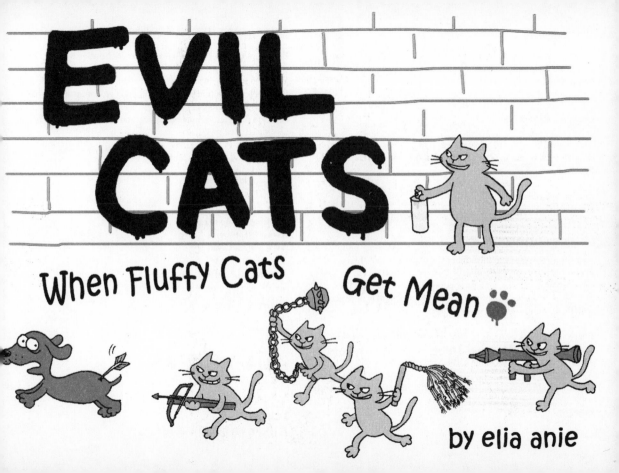

To Penn

When she is not fleeing from all things feline, Elia Anie likes to ponder on things of consequence. She currently lives in a giant litter box in the U.S.

First published in 2009 by
HEADLINE PUBLISHING GROUP

1

Cataloguing in Publication Data is available from the British Library

ISBN 978 0 7553 6002 4

Typeset by Avon DataSet Ltd, Bidford-on-Avon, Warwickshire

Printed in the UK by CPI William Clowes Beccles NR34 7TL

Headline's policy is to use papers that are natural, renewable and recyclable products and made from wood grown in sustainable forests. The logging and manufacturing processes are expected to conform to the environmental regulations of the country of origin.

HEADLINE PUBLISHING GROUP
An Hachette Livre UK Company
338 Euston Road
London NW1 3BH

www.headline.co.uk
www.hachettelivre.co.uk
www.evilcats.co.uk
www.evil-cats.com

Also available from Headline

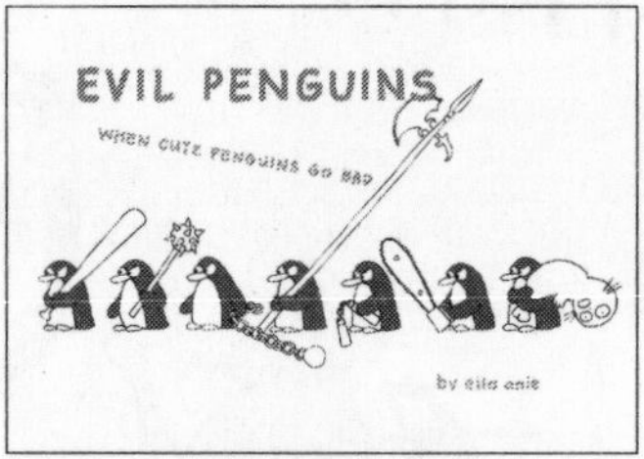
EVIL PENGUINS
WHEN CUTE PENGUINS GO BAD
by elia anie

Evil Penguins
ISBN 978 0 7553 1804 9

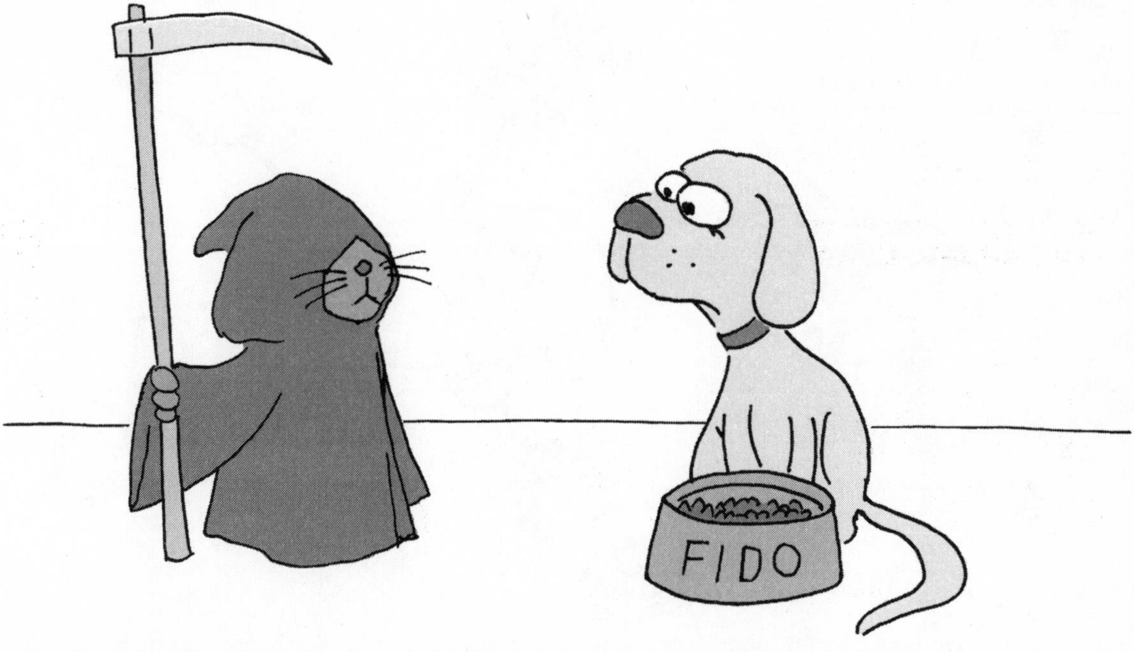
FIDO

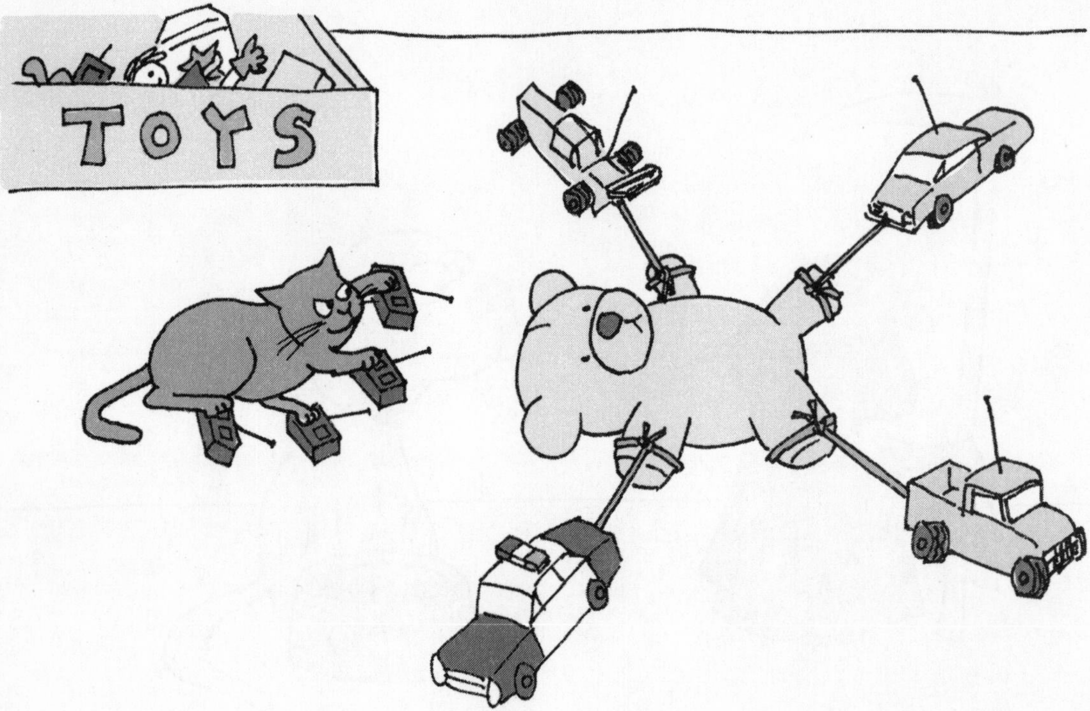
TOYS

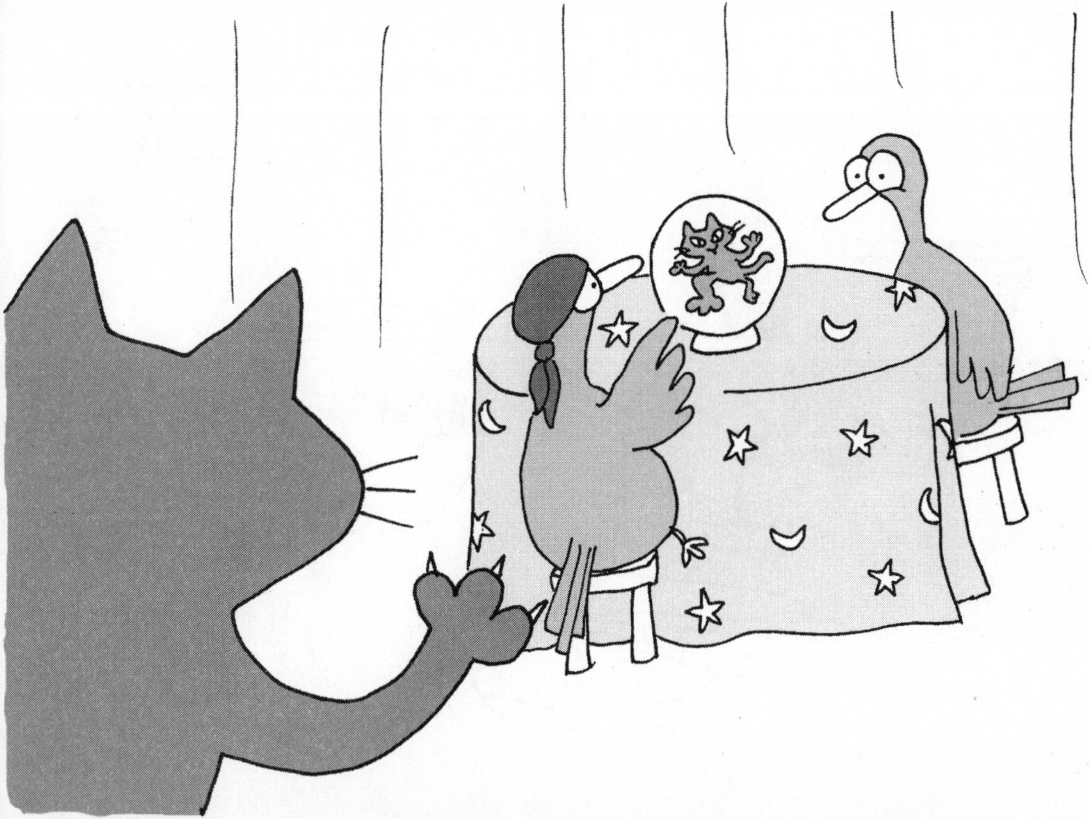

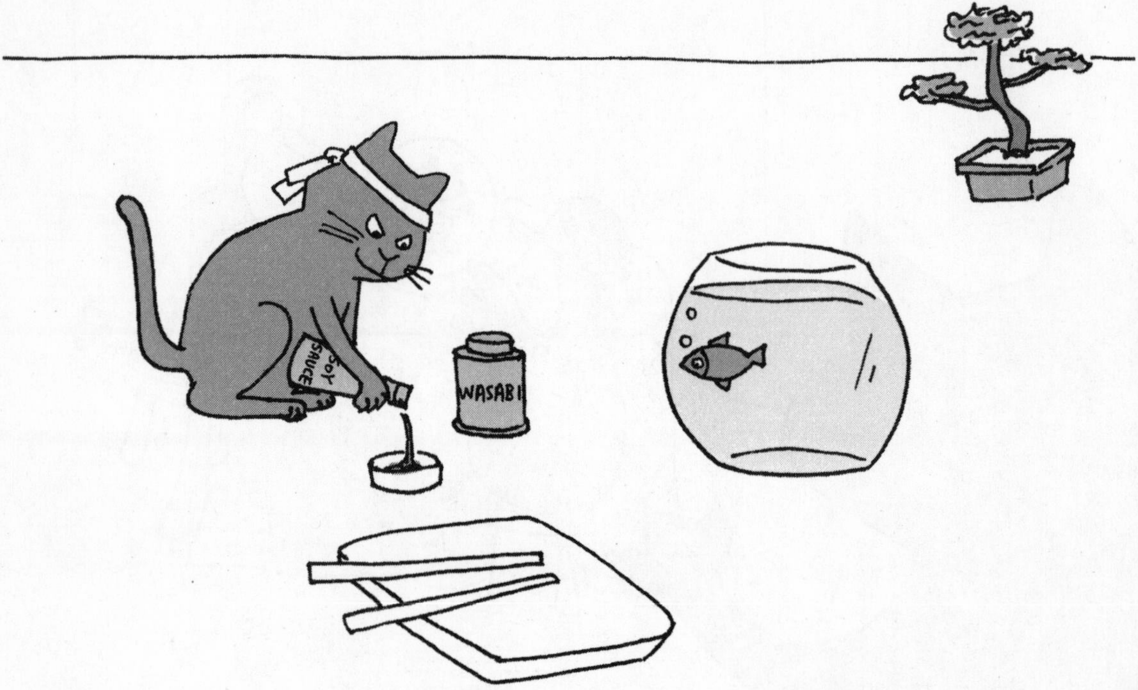
SOY SAUCE
WASABI

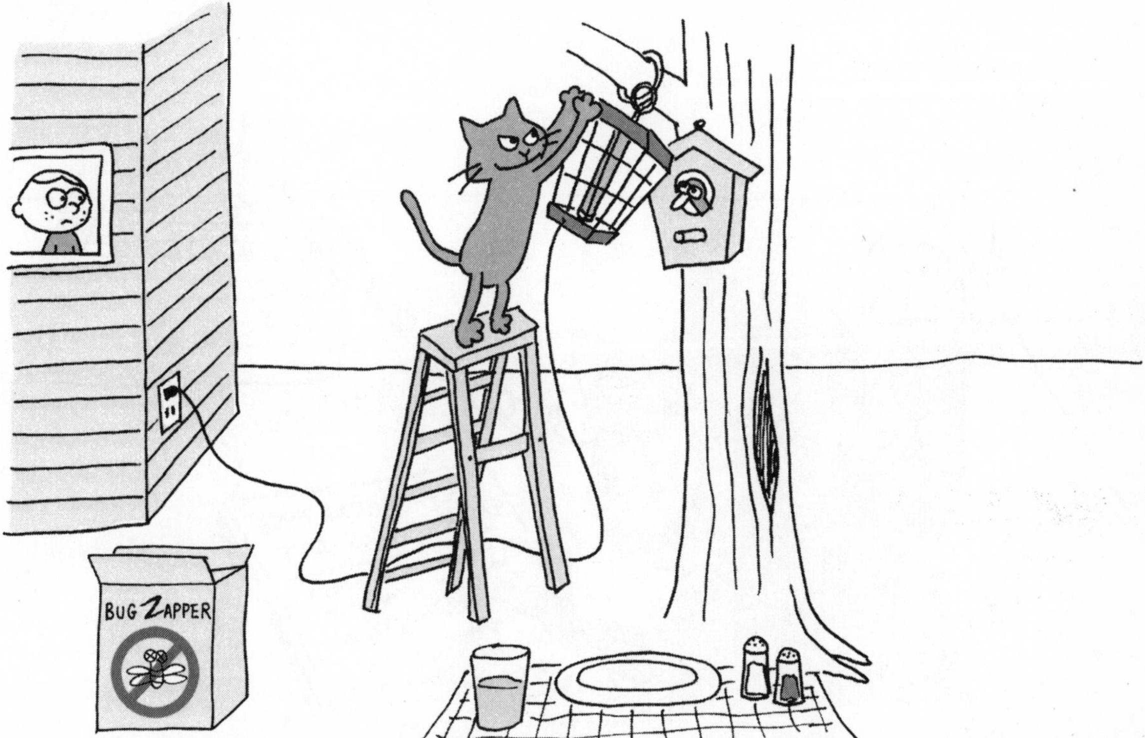
BUG ZAPPER

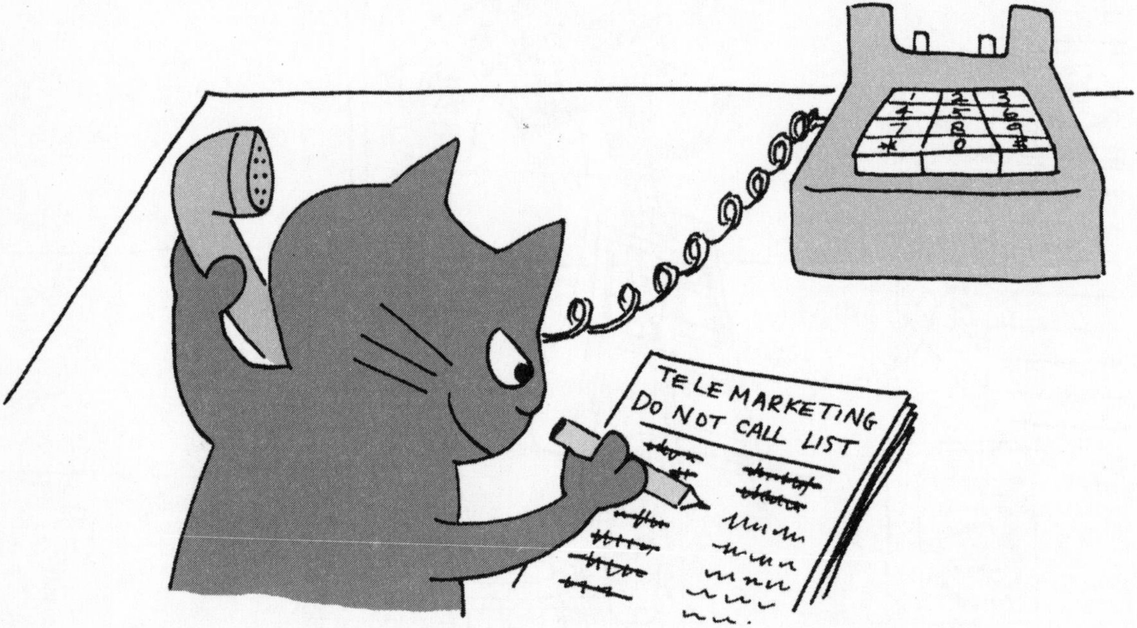
TELEMARKETING
DO NOT CALL LIST

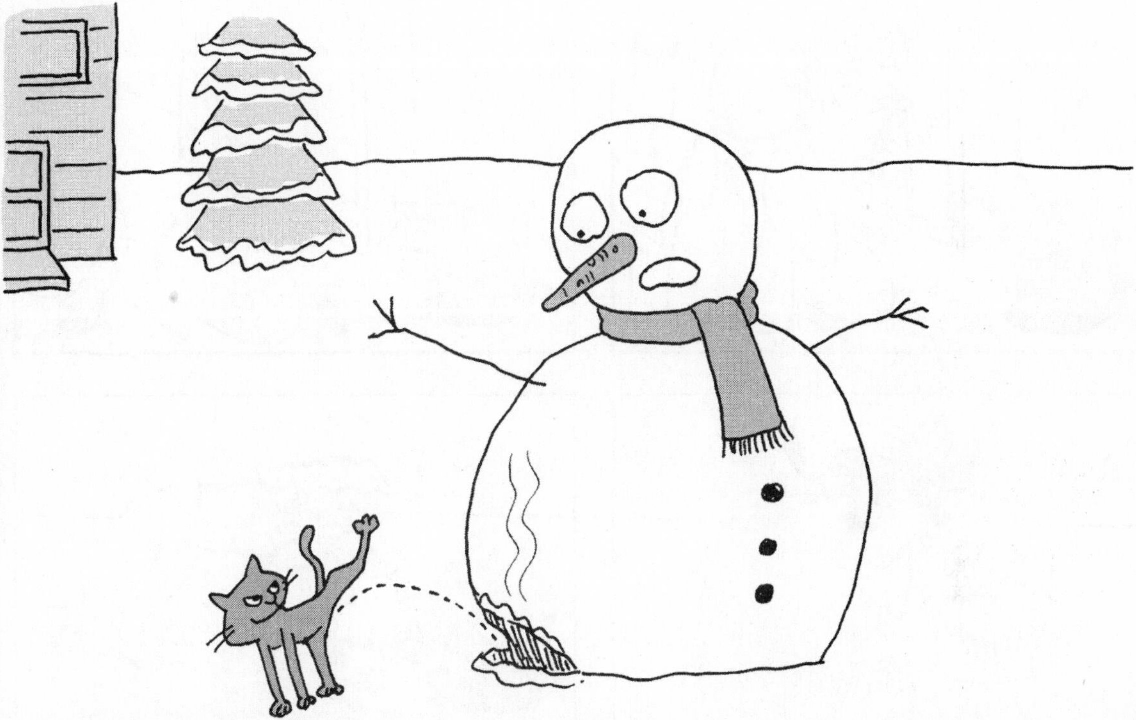

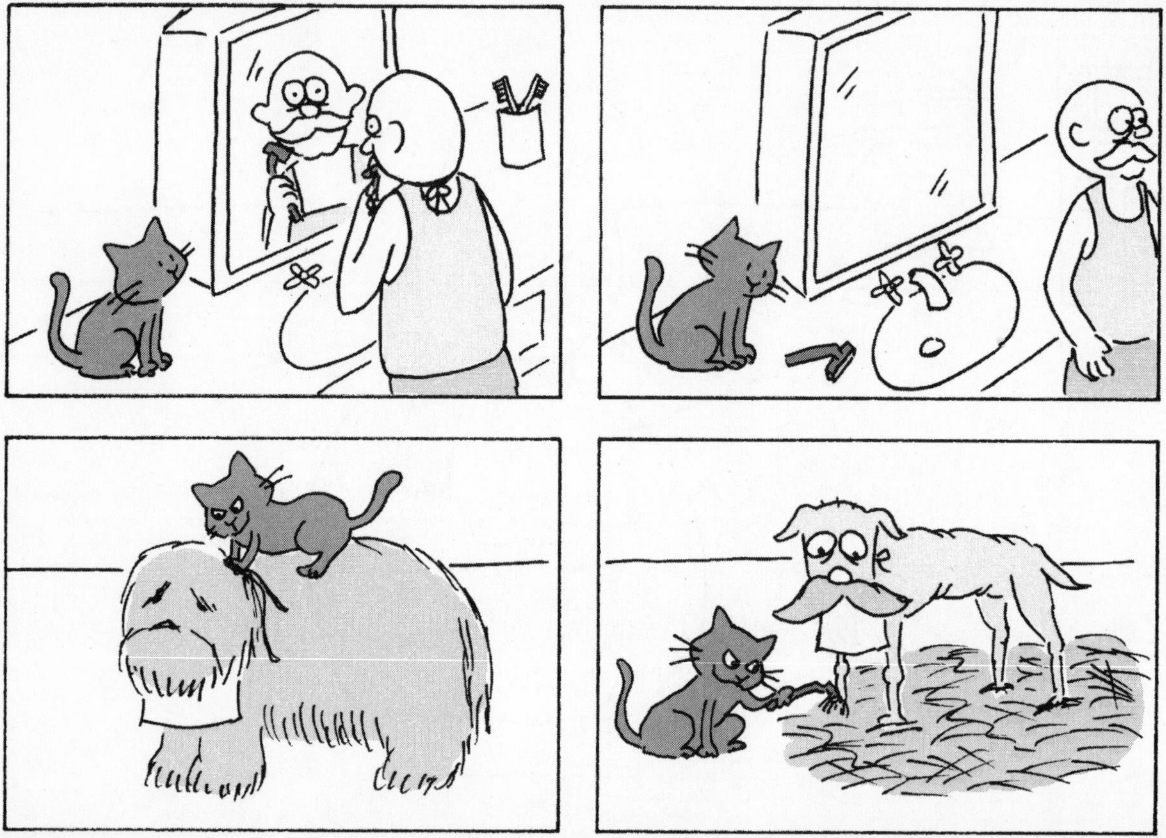

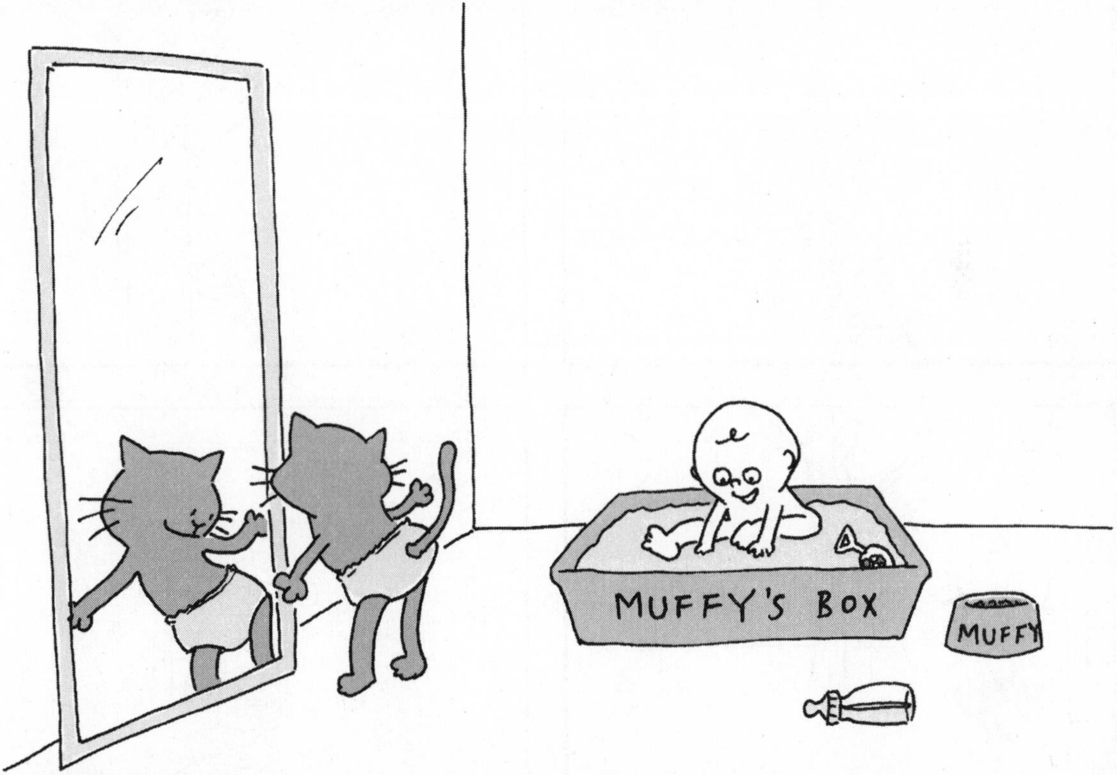
MUFFY'S BOX
MUFFY

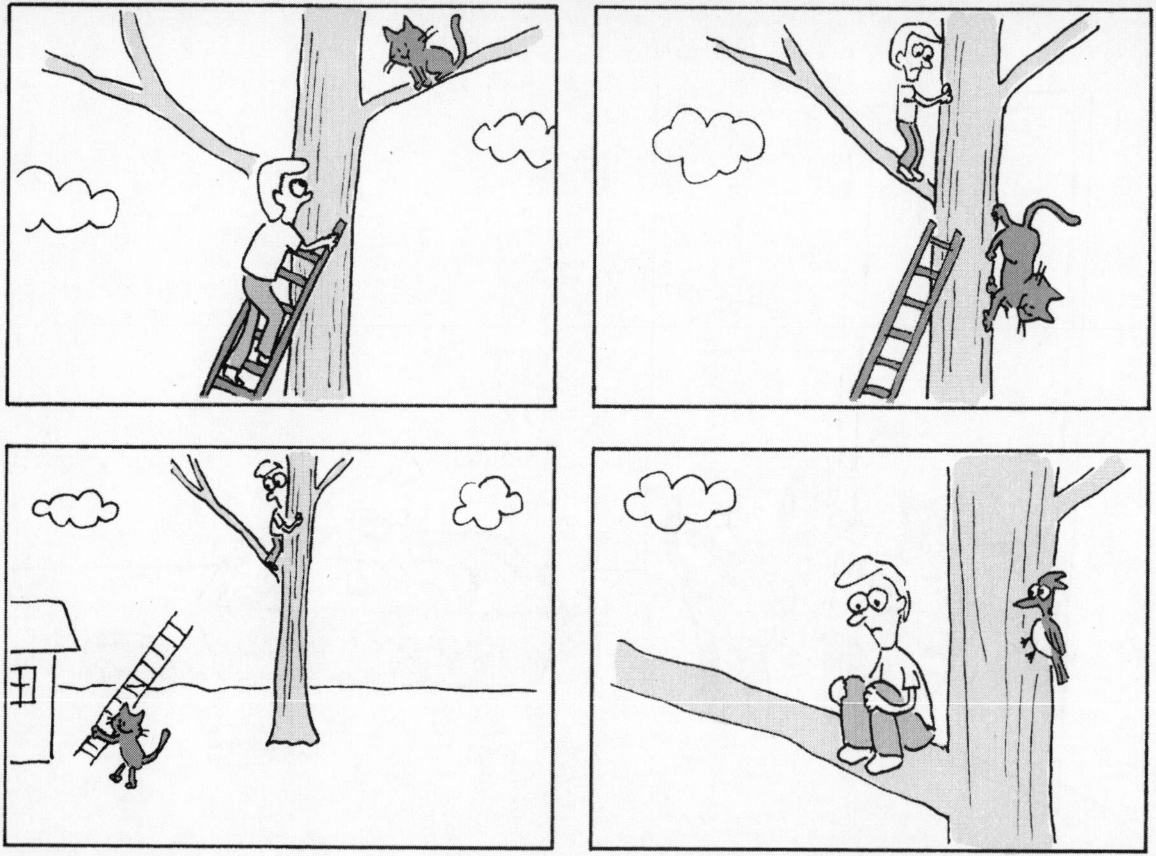

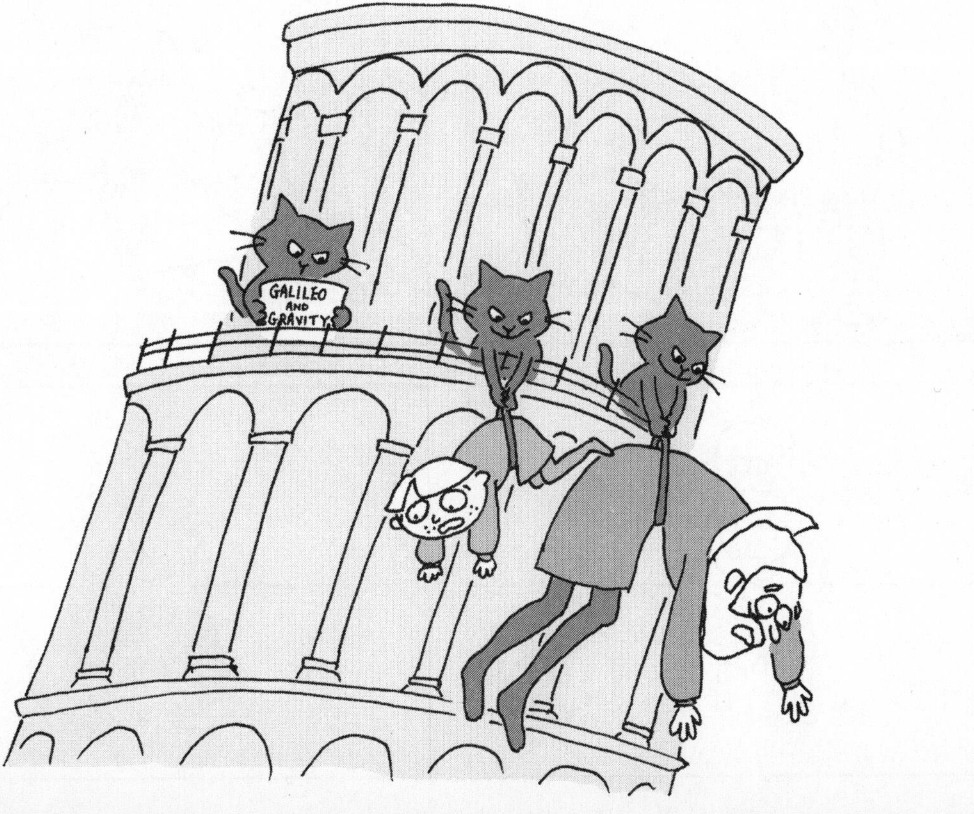
GALILEO AND GRAVITY

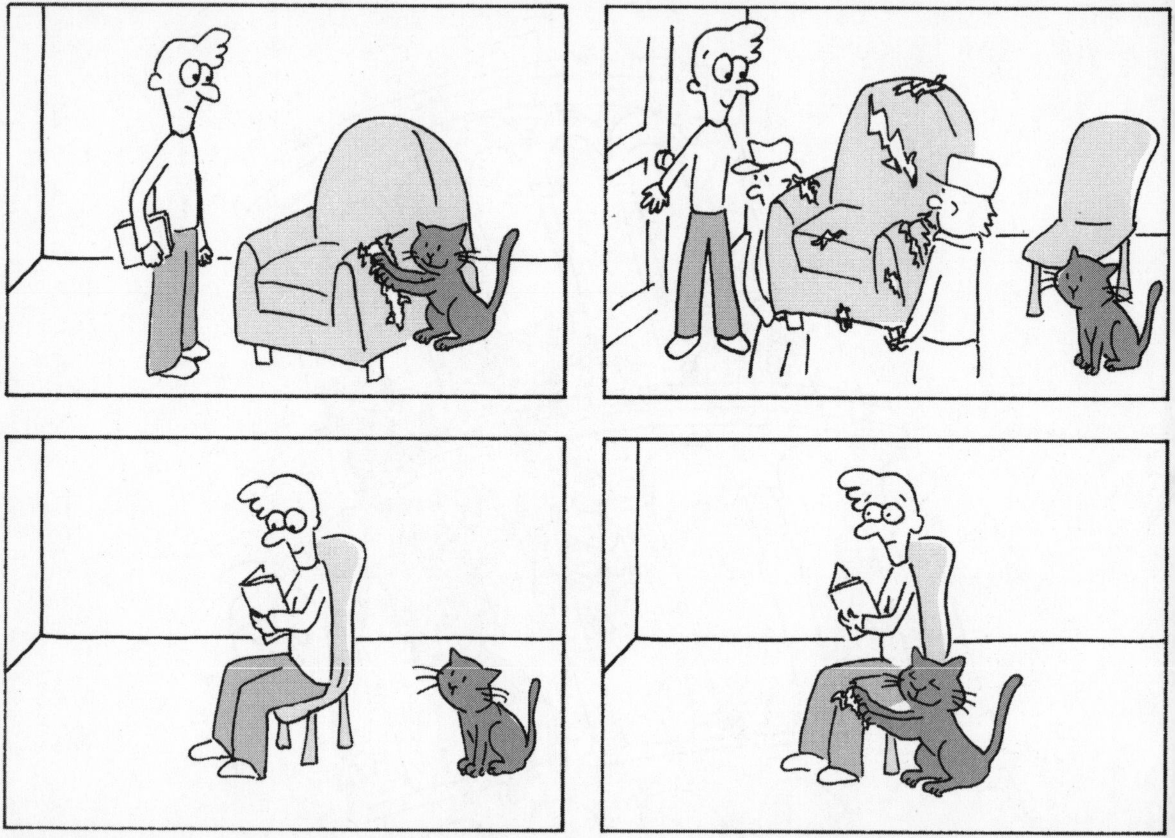

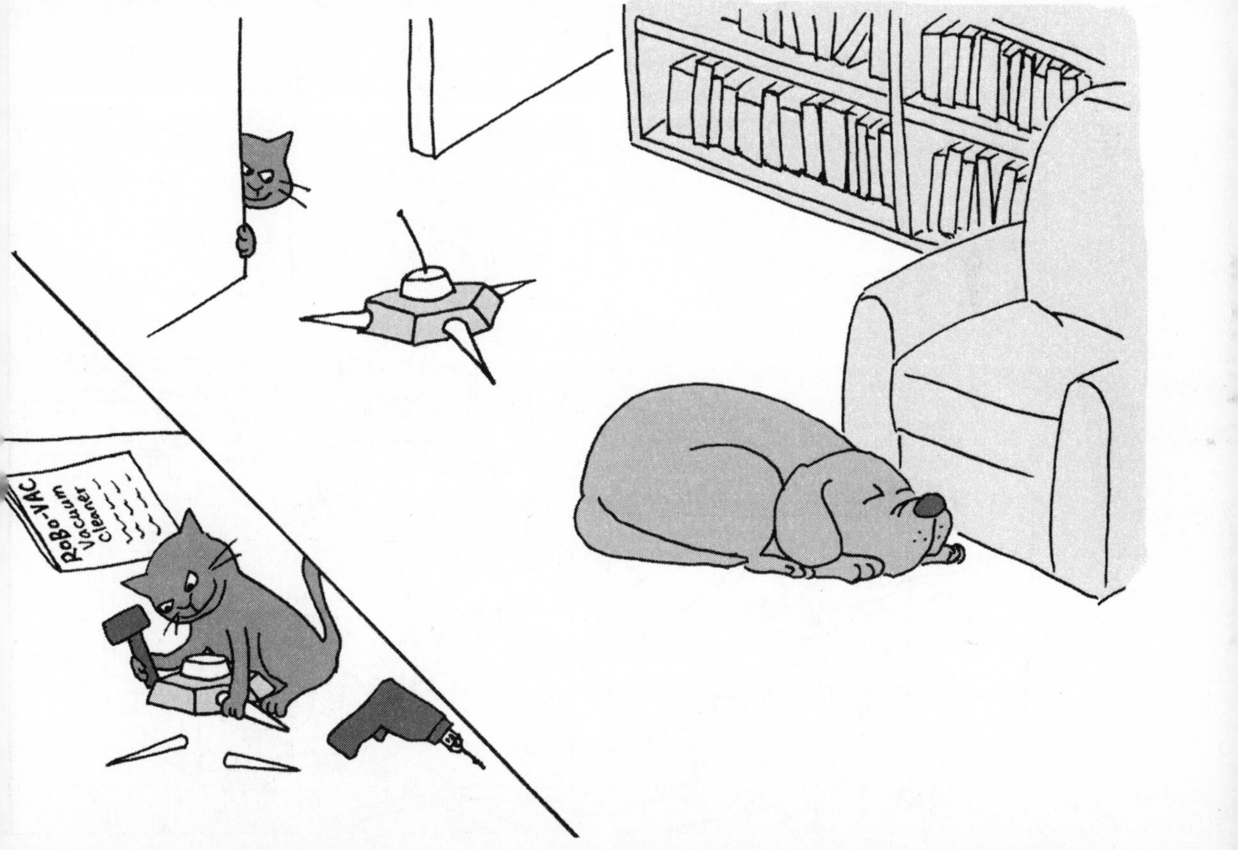
RoBo-VAC
Vacuum
Cleaner

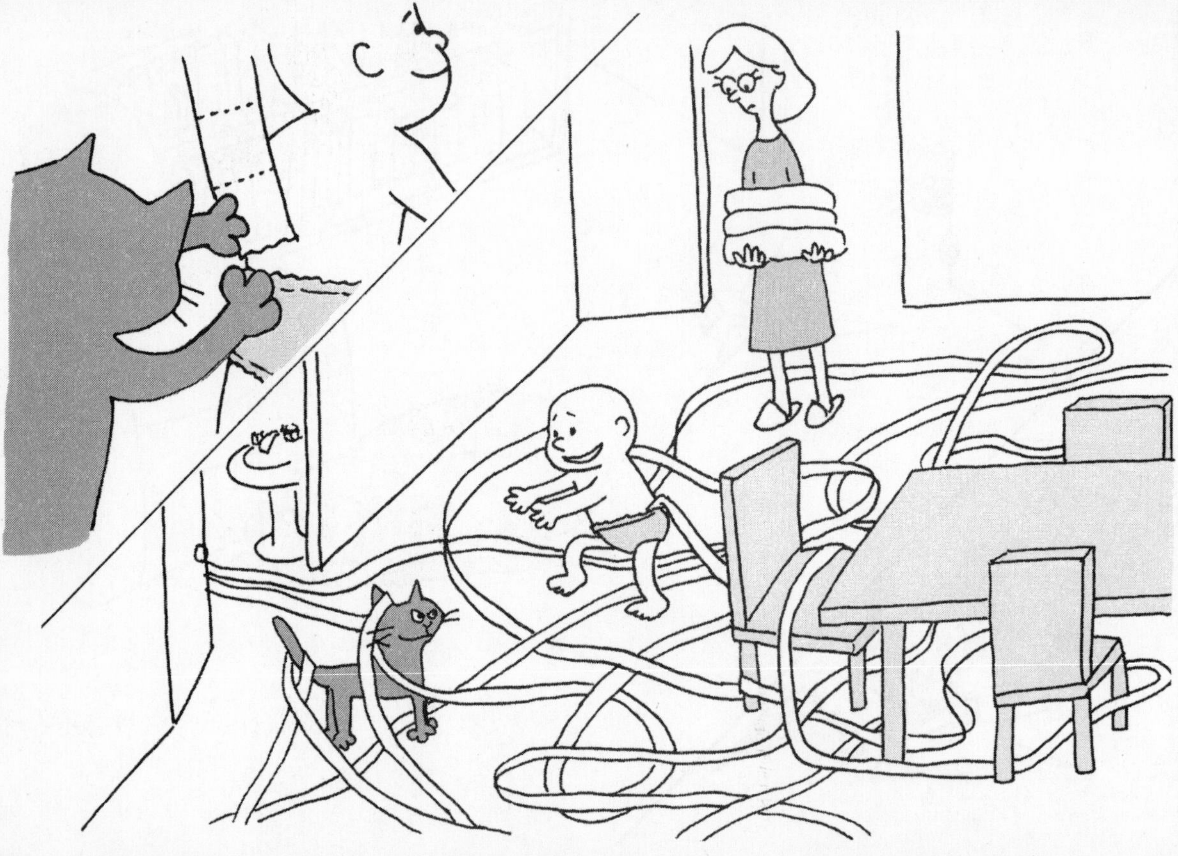

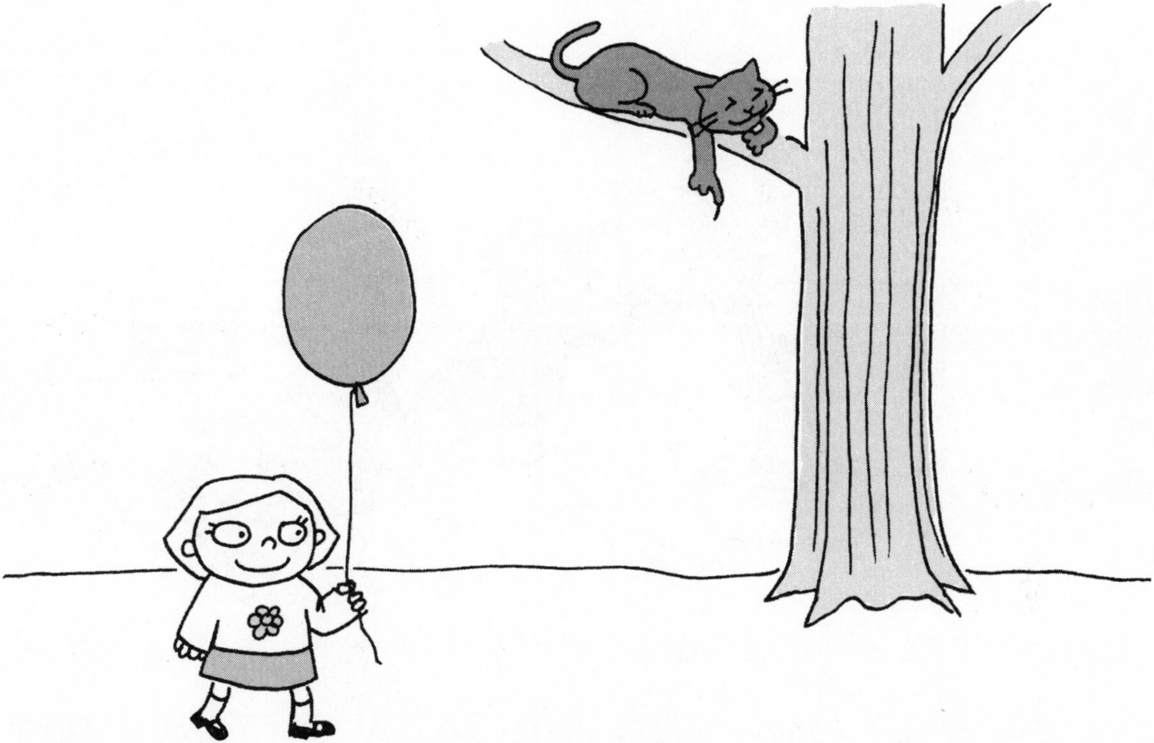

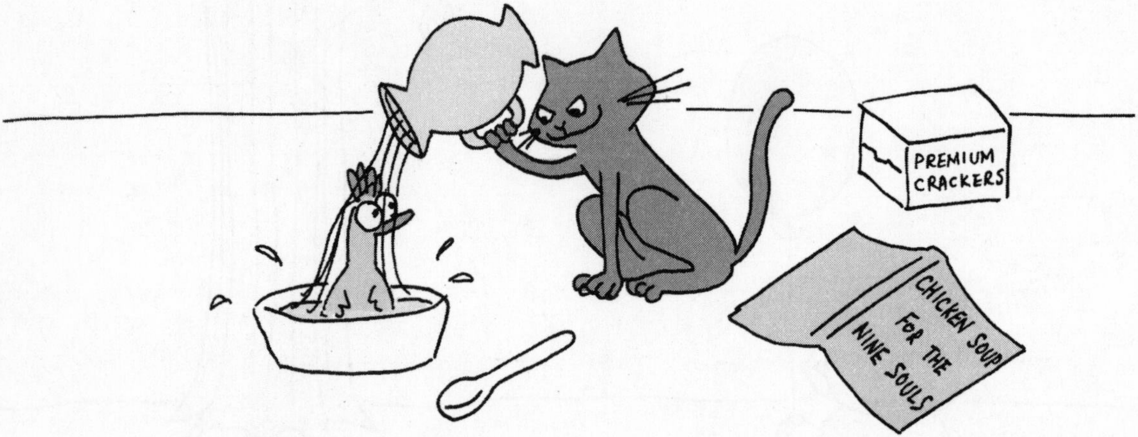
PREMIUM CRACKERS
CHICKEN SOUP FOR THE NINE SOULS

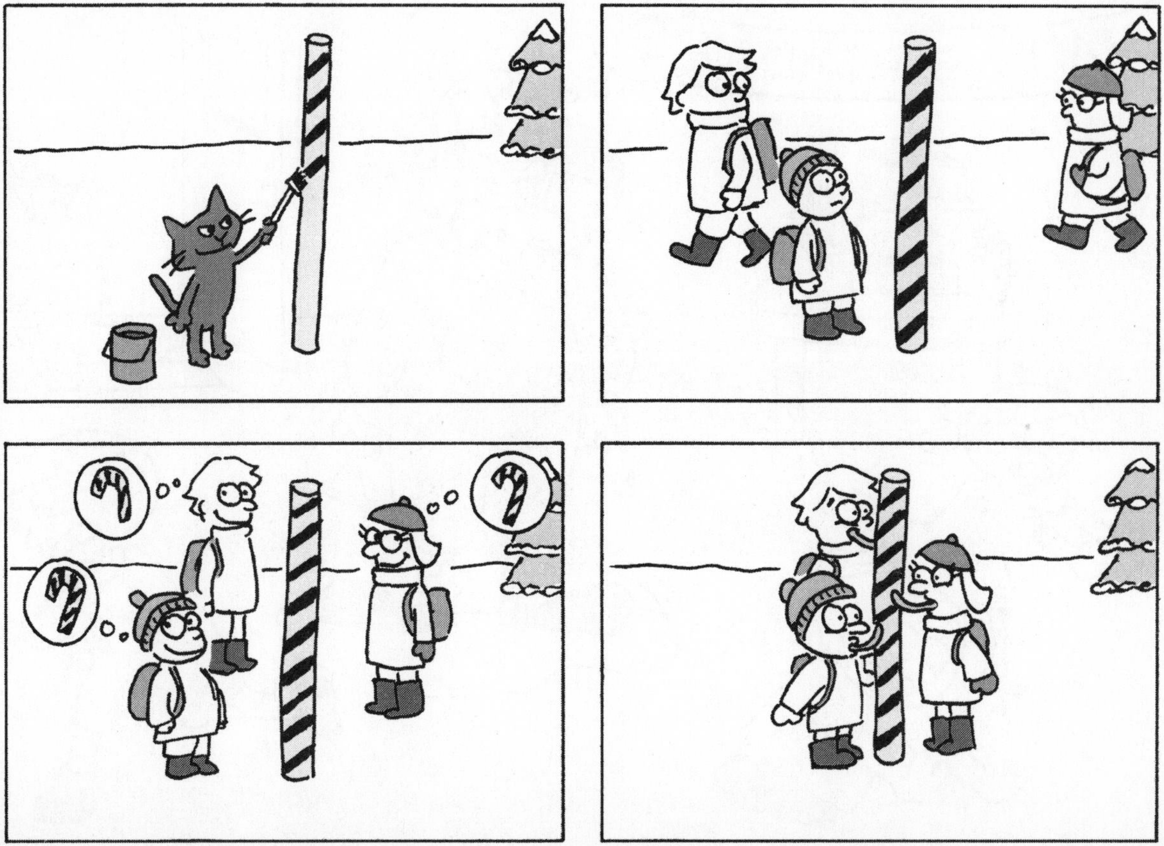

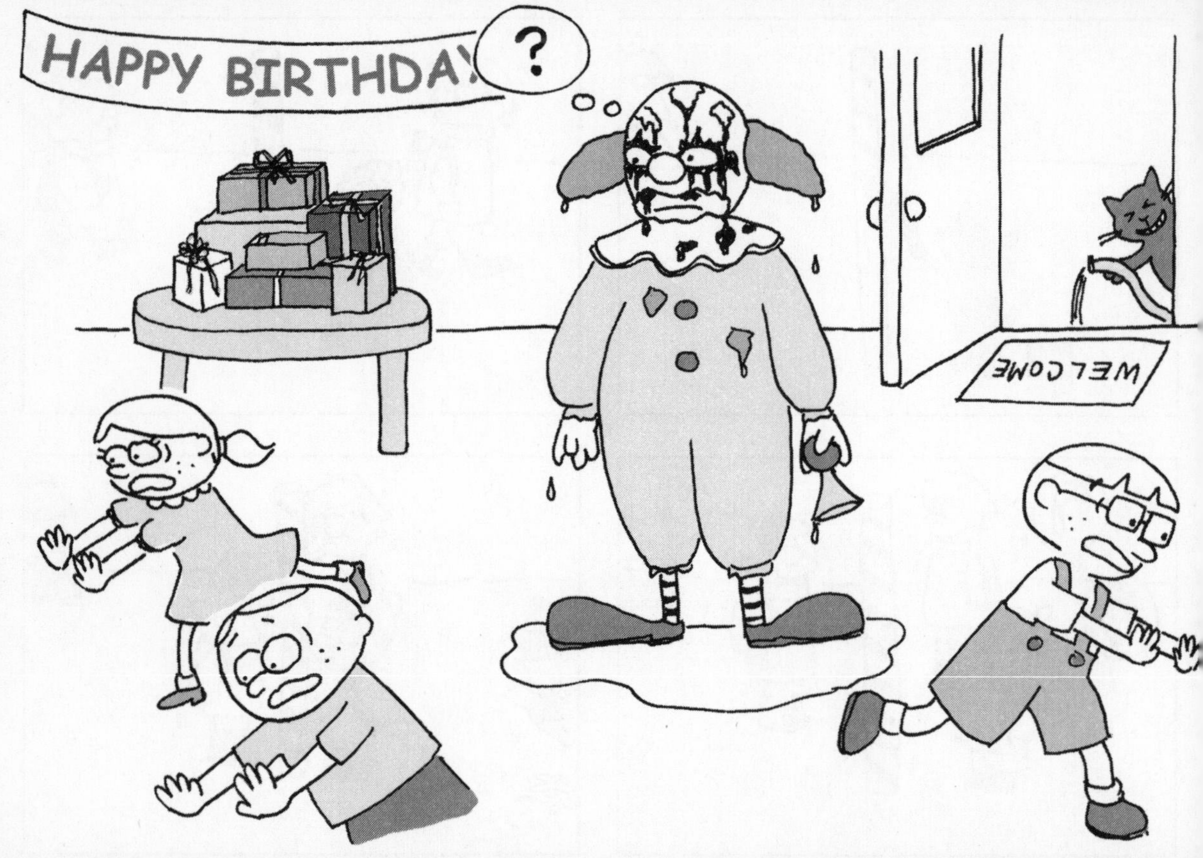
HAPPY BIRTHDAY
?
WELCOME

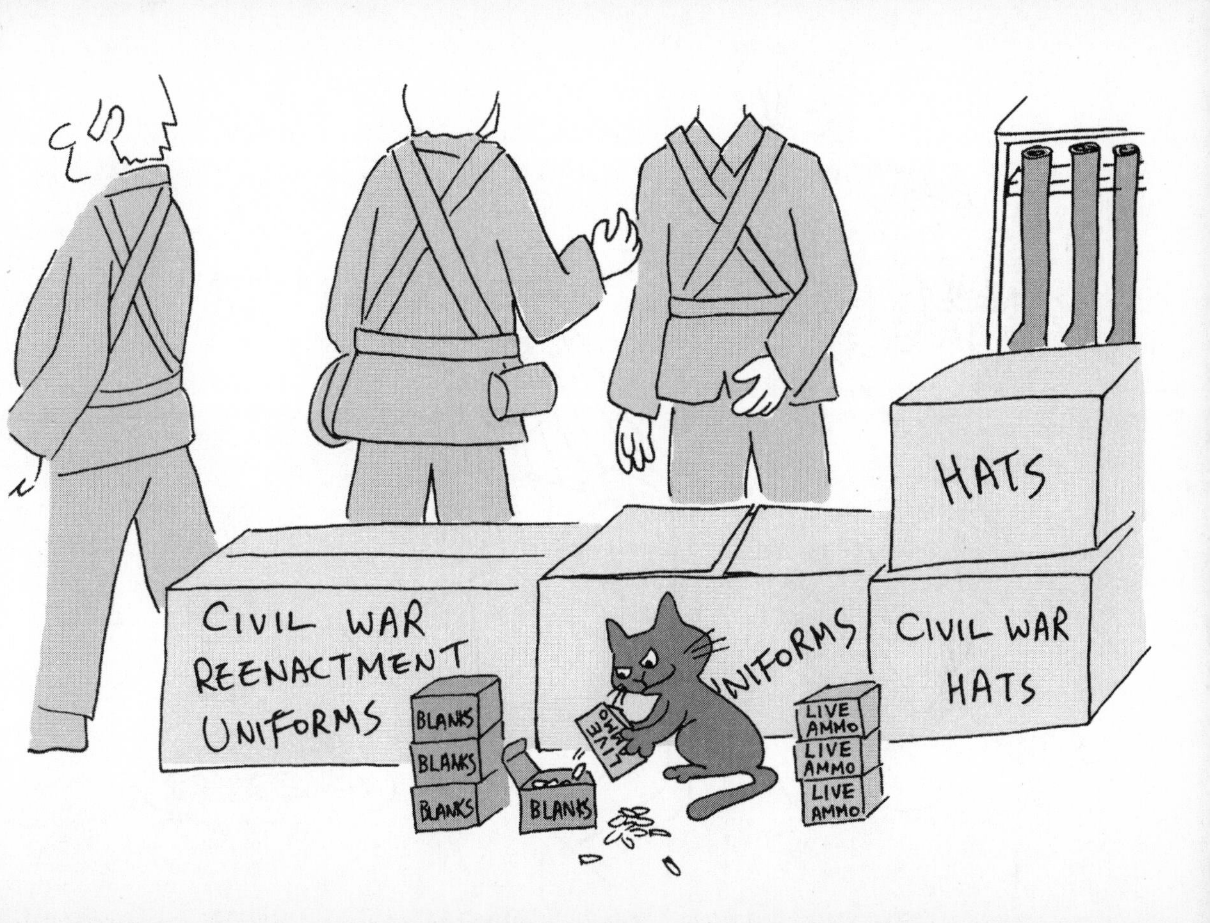
HATS
CIVIL WAR REENACTMENT UNIFORMS
UNIFORMS
CIVIL WAR HATS
BLANKS
BLANKS
BLANKS
BLANKS
LIVE AMMO
LIVE AMMO
LIVE AMMO
LIVE AMMO

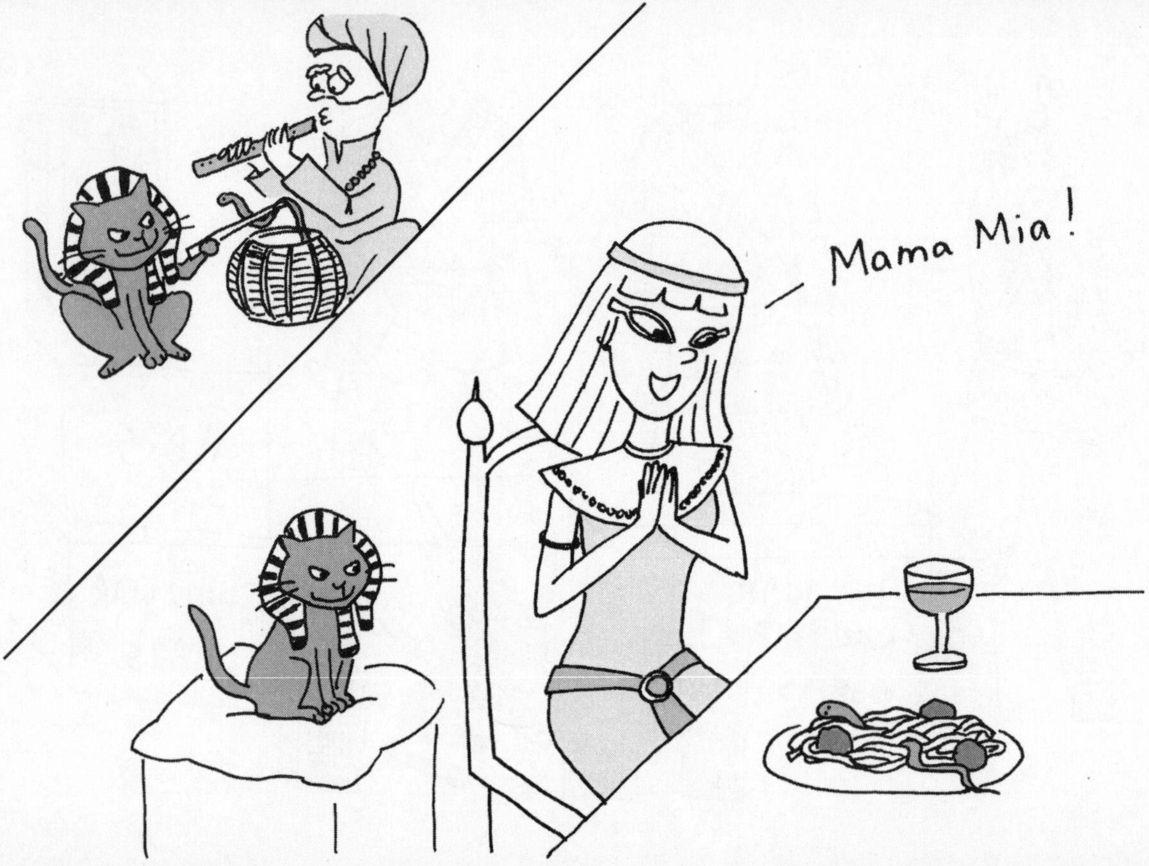
Mama Mia!

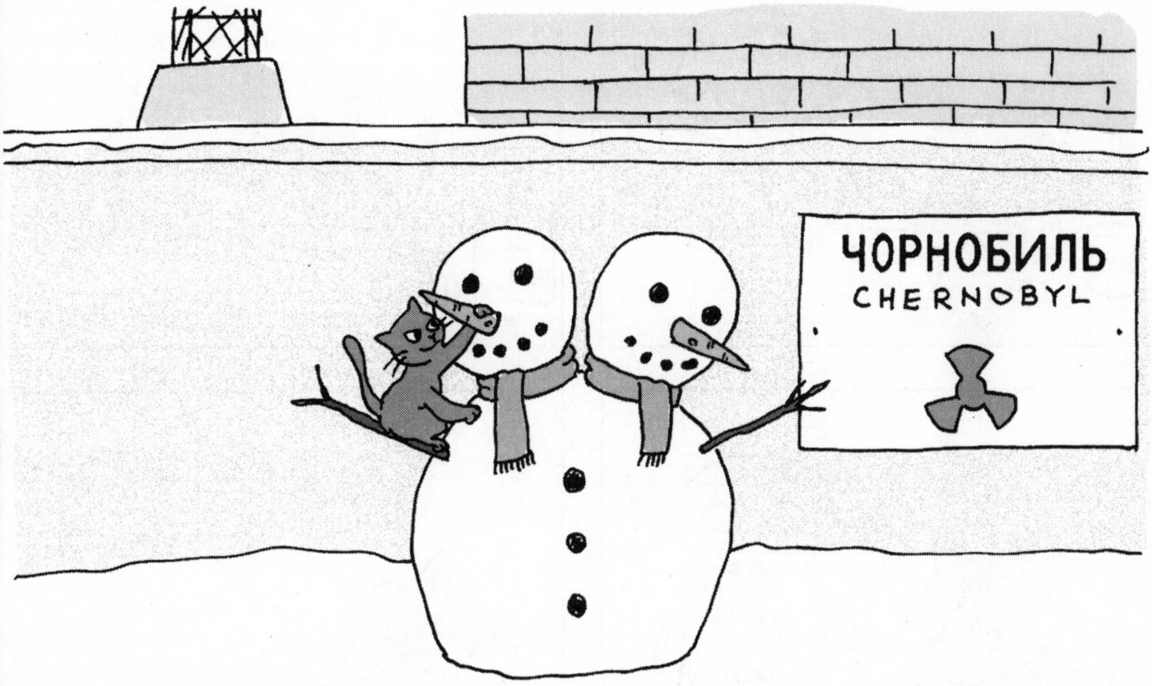
ЧОРНОБИЛЬ
CHERNOBYL

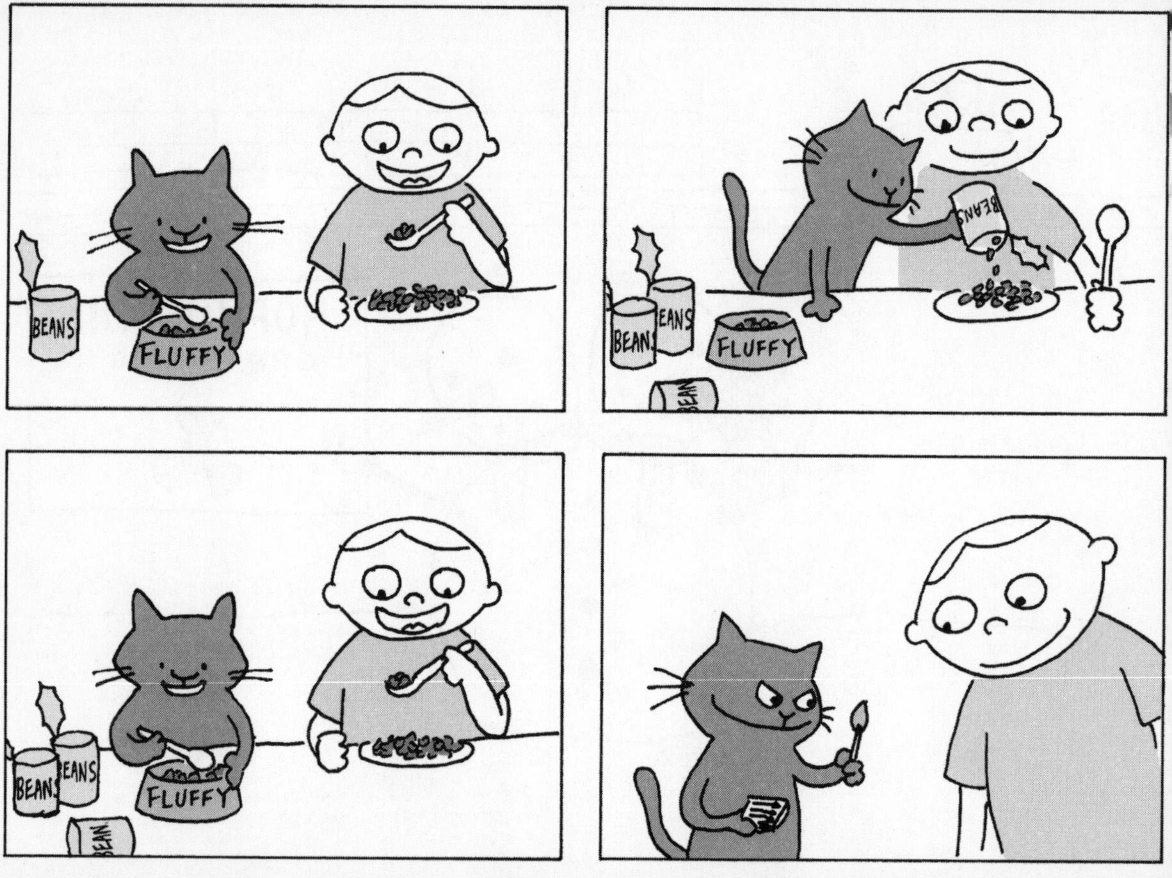
BEANS
FLUFFY
BEANS
EANS
FLUFFY
BEANS
EANS
FLUFFY

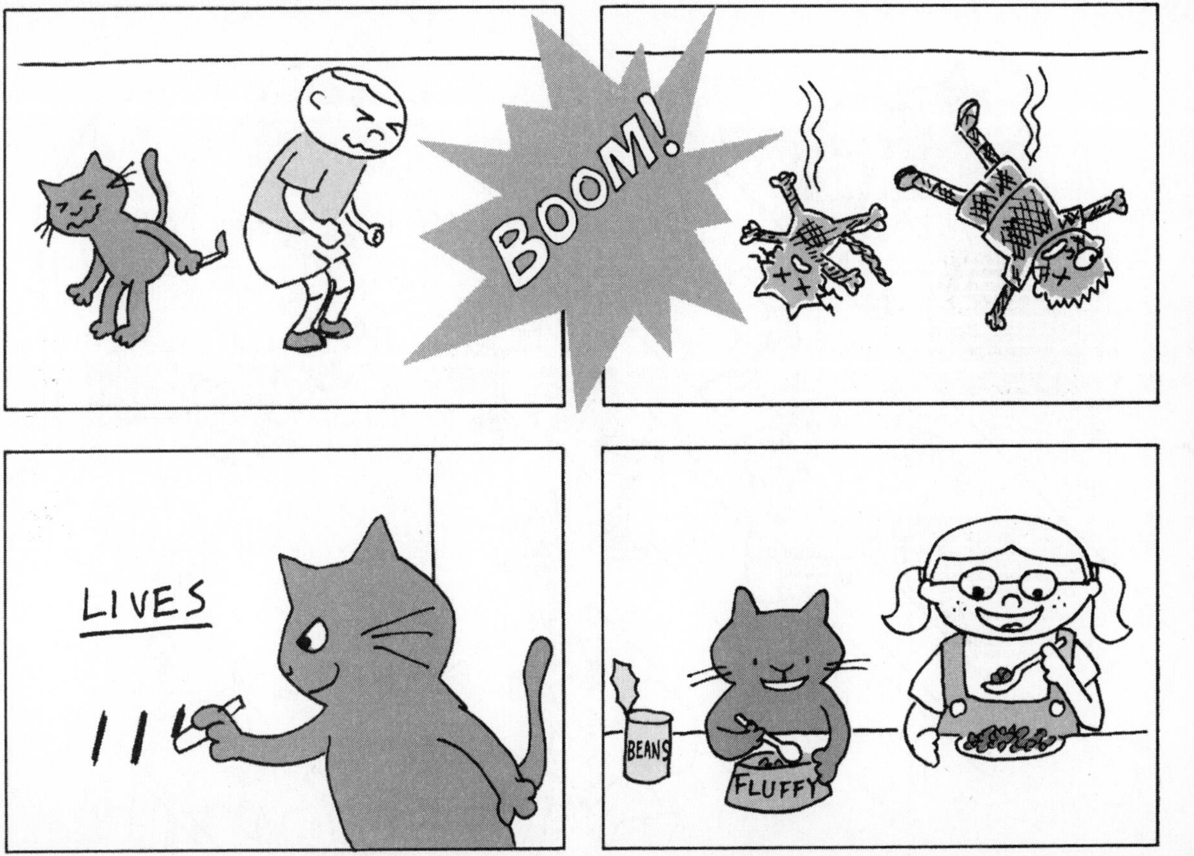
BOOM!
LIVES
BEANS
FLUFFY

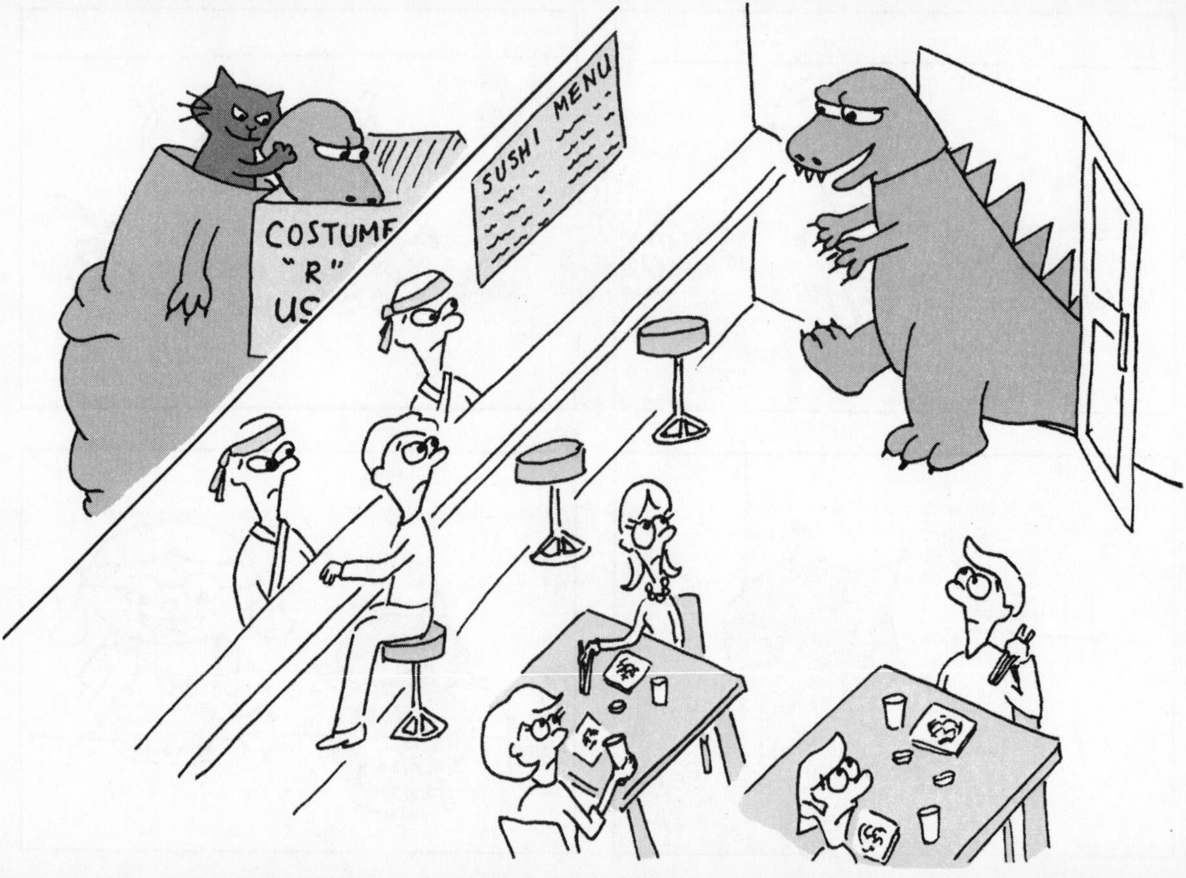
COSTUME "R" US
SUSHI MENU

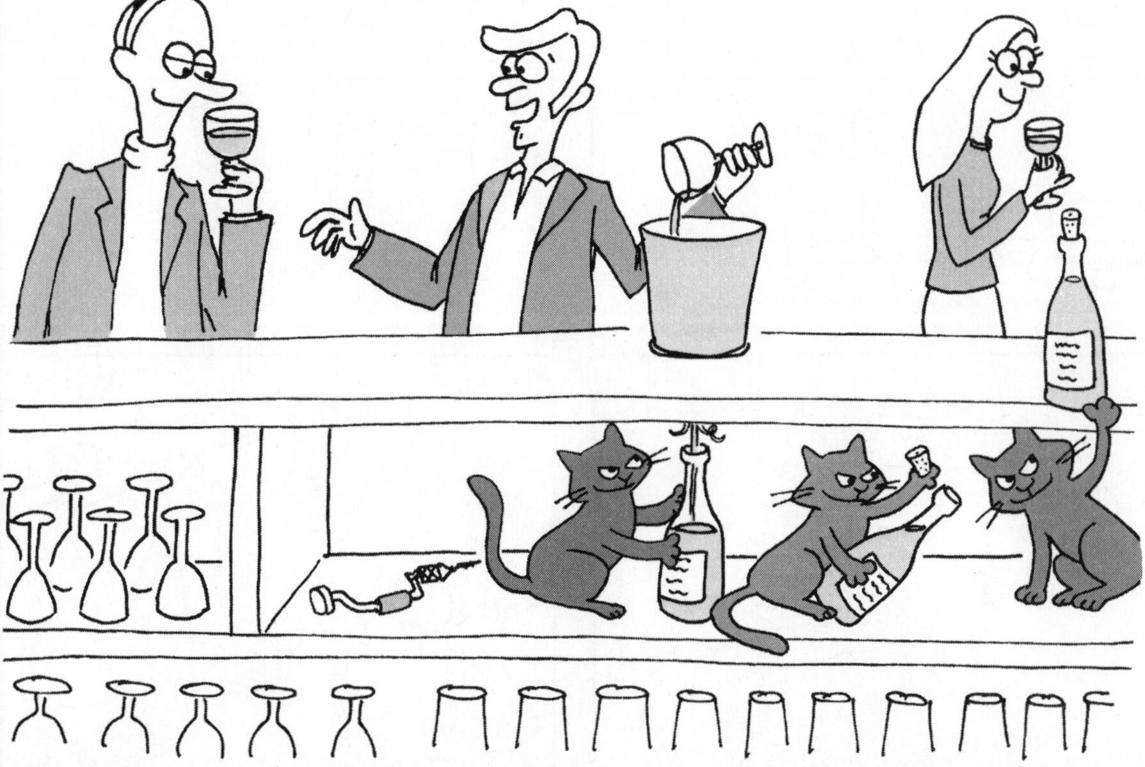

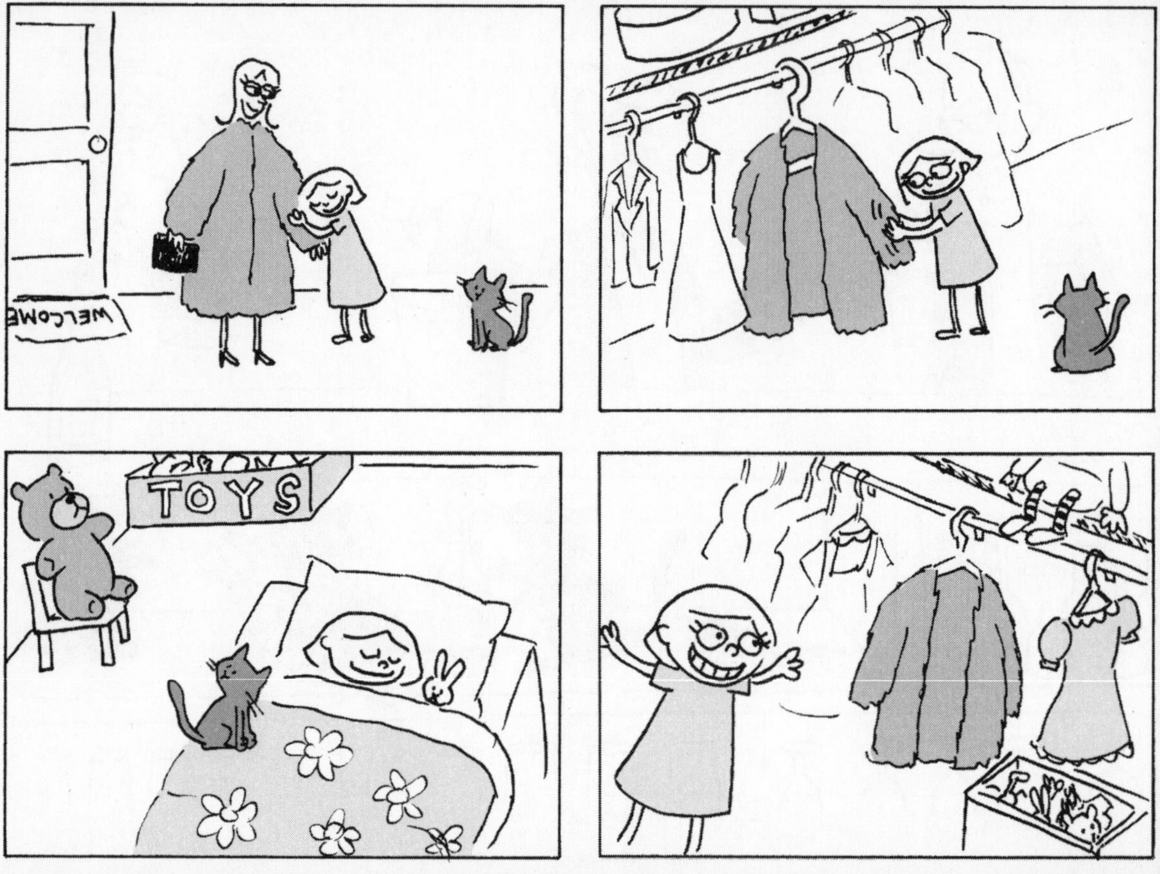
WELCOME
TOYS

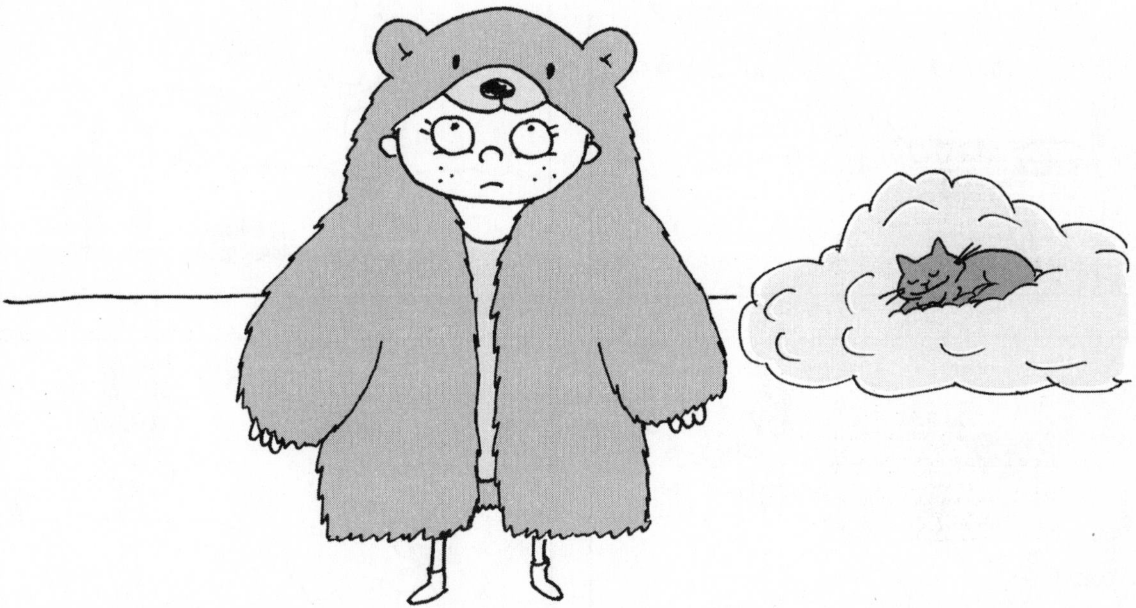

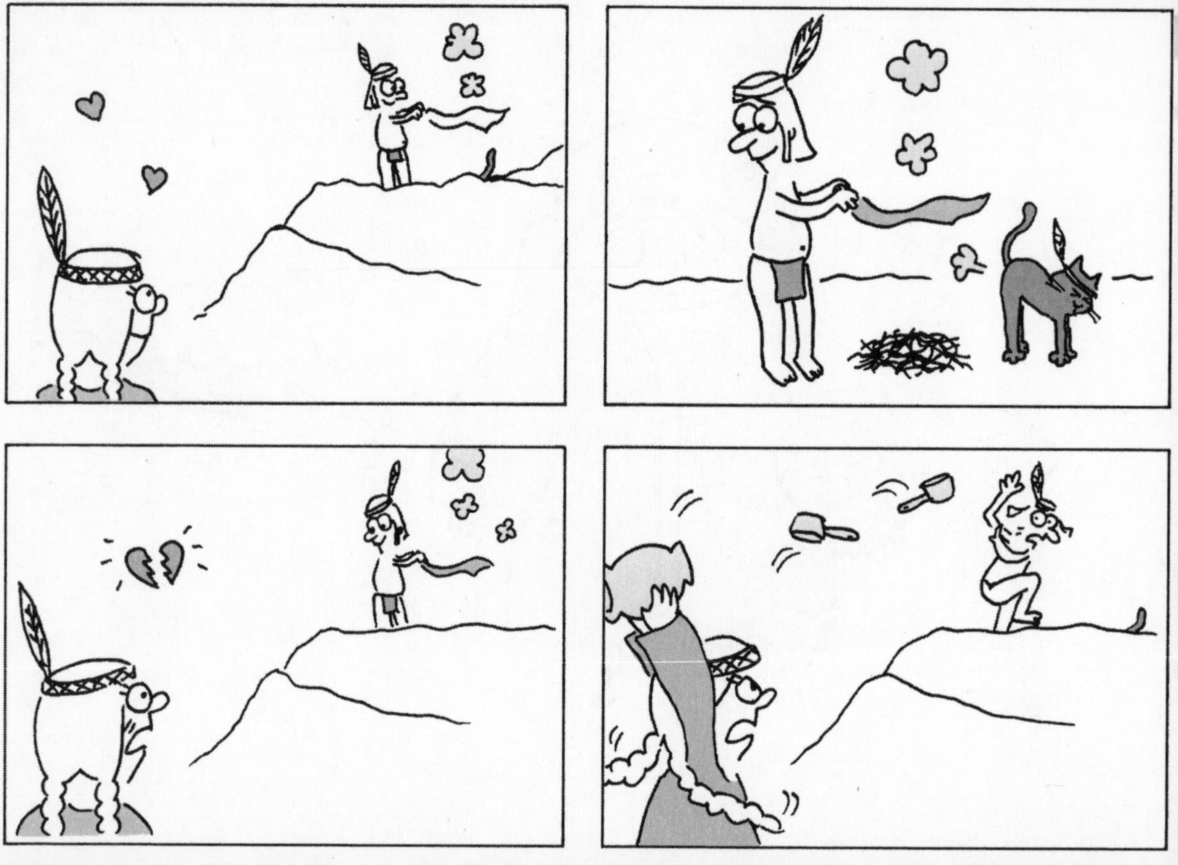

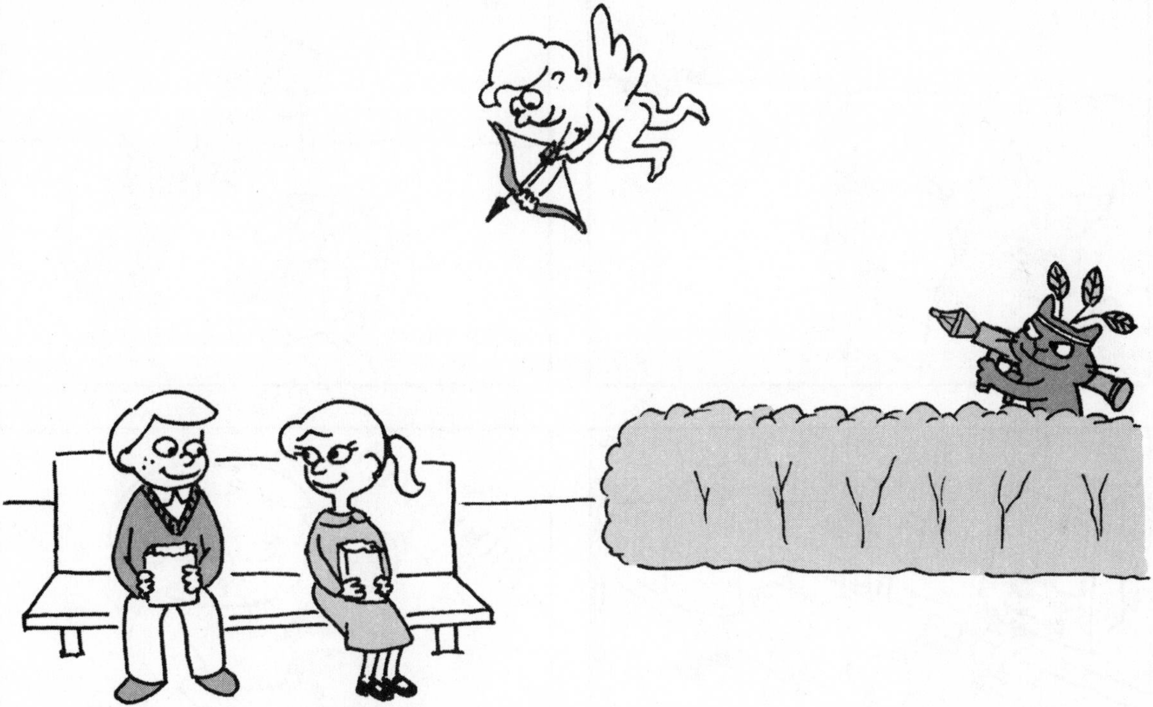

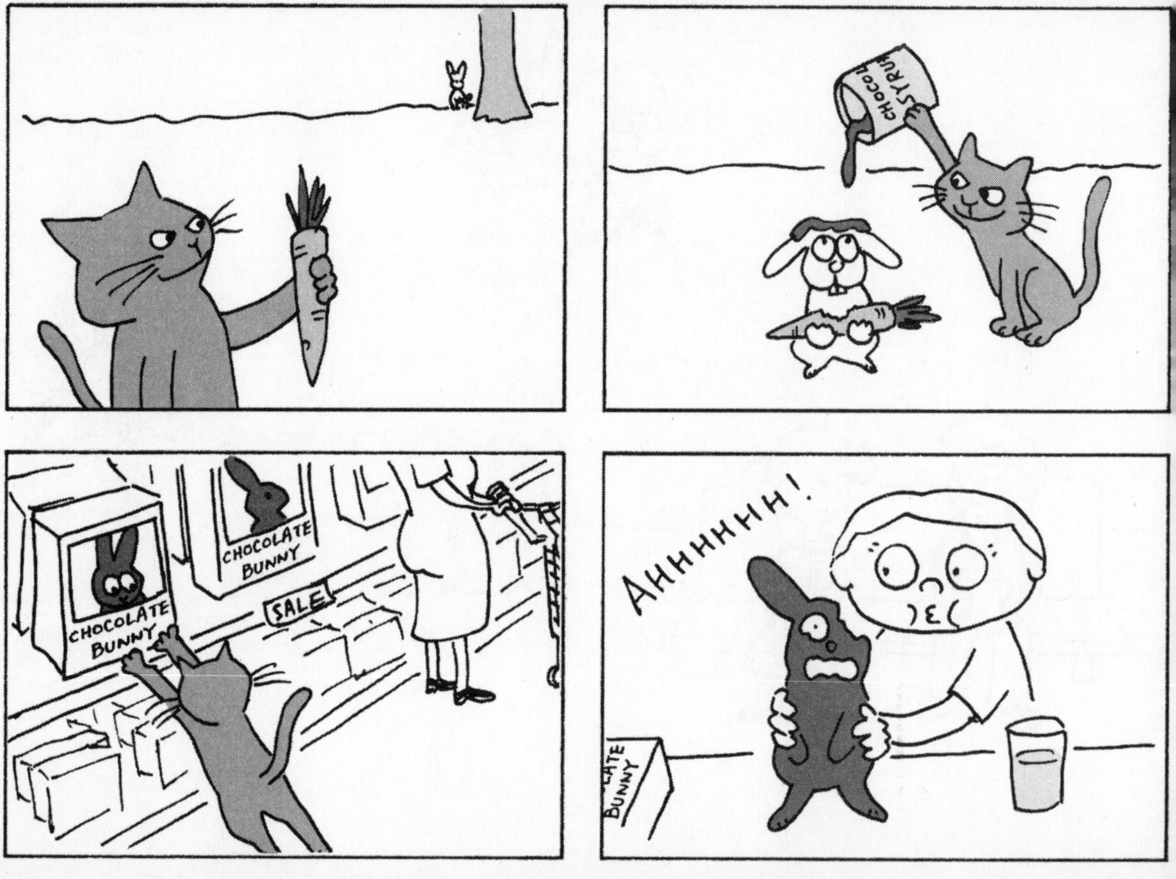
CHOCO
SYRU
CHOCOLATE BUNNY
CHOCOLATE BUNNY
SALE
AHHHHHH!
LATE BUNNY

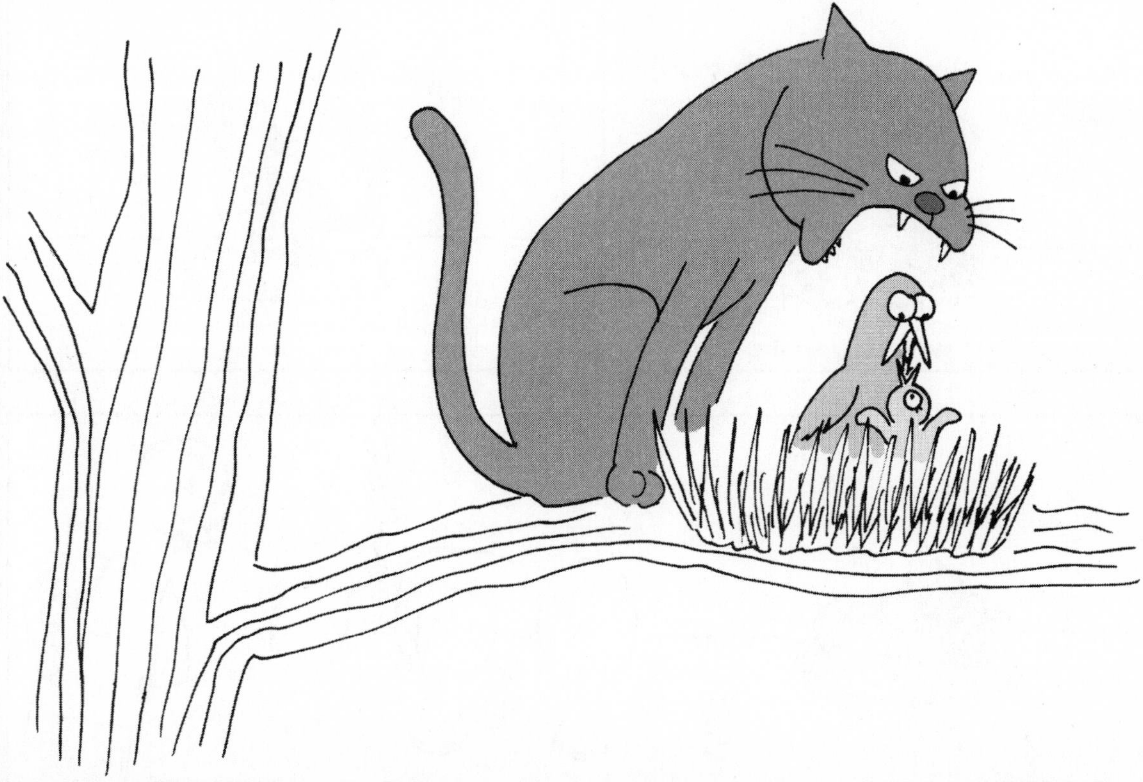

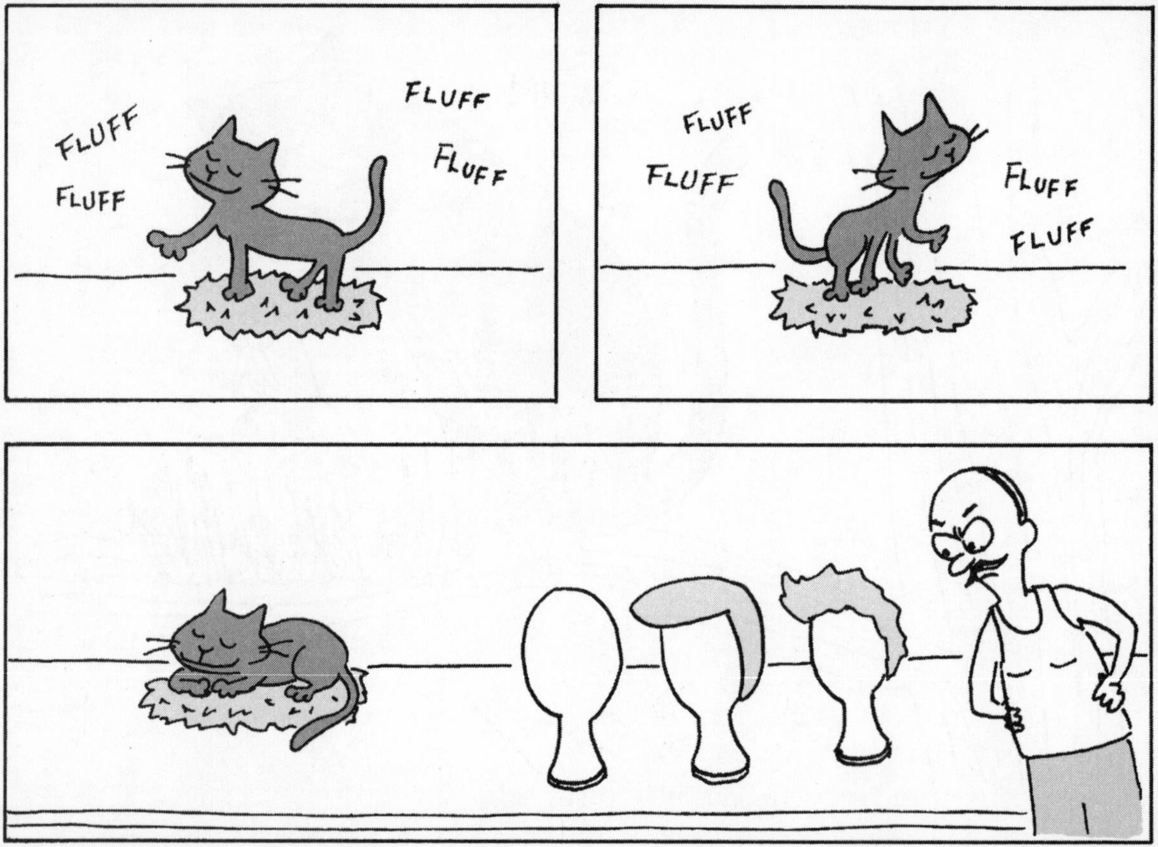

FLUFF
FLUFF
FLUFF
FLUFF
FLUFF
FLUFF
FLUFF
FLUFF

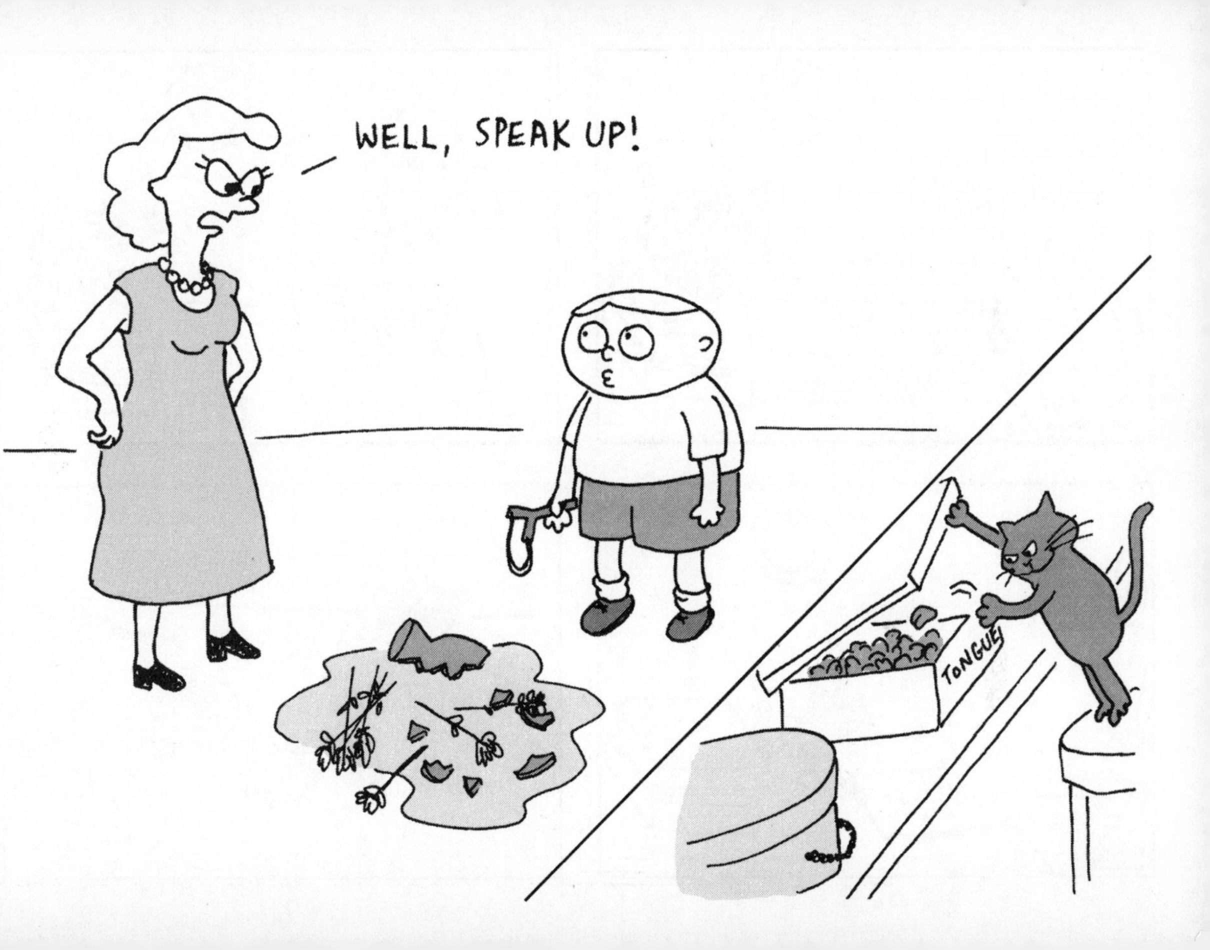
WELL, SPEAK UP!
TONGUE

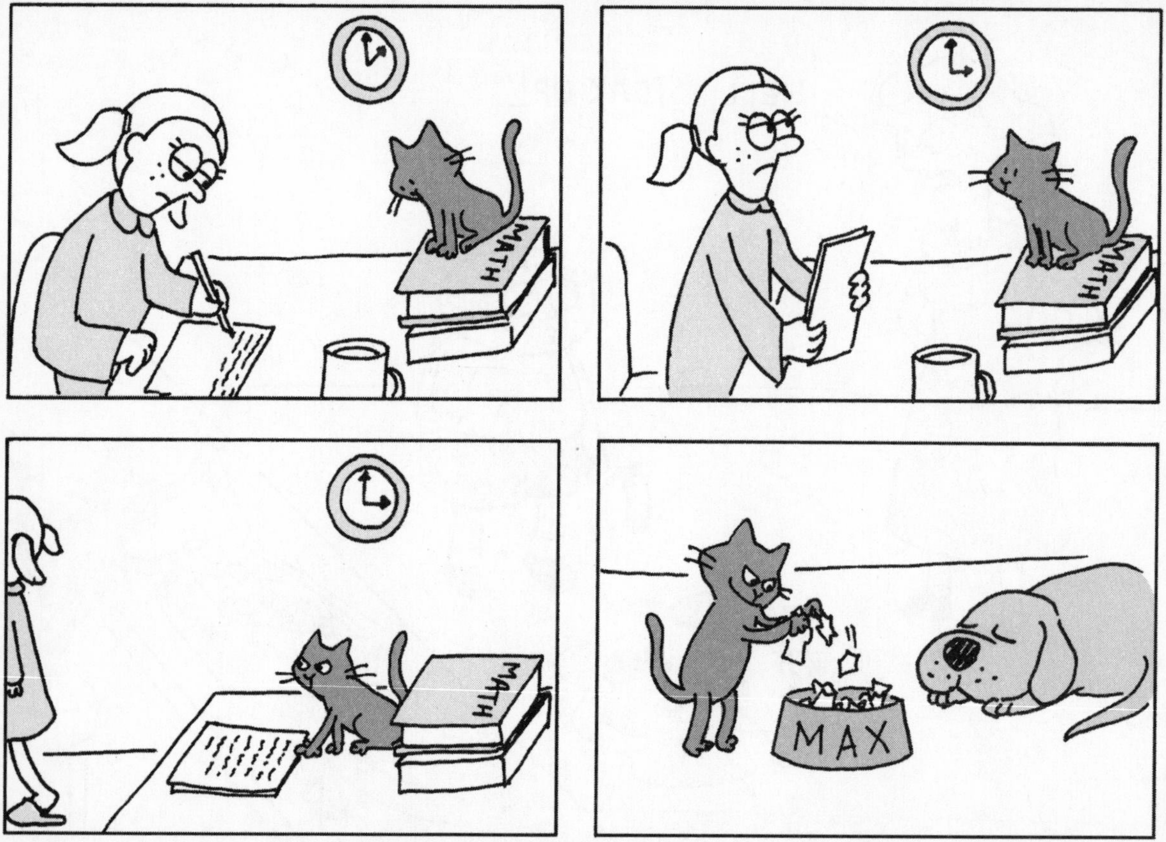
MATH
MATH
MATH
MAX

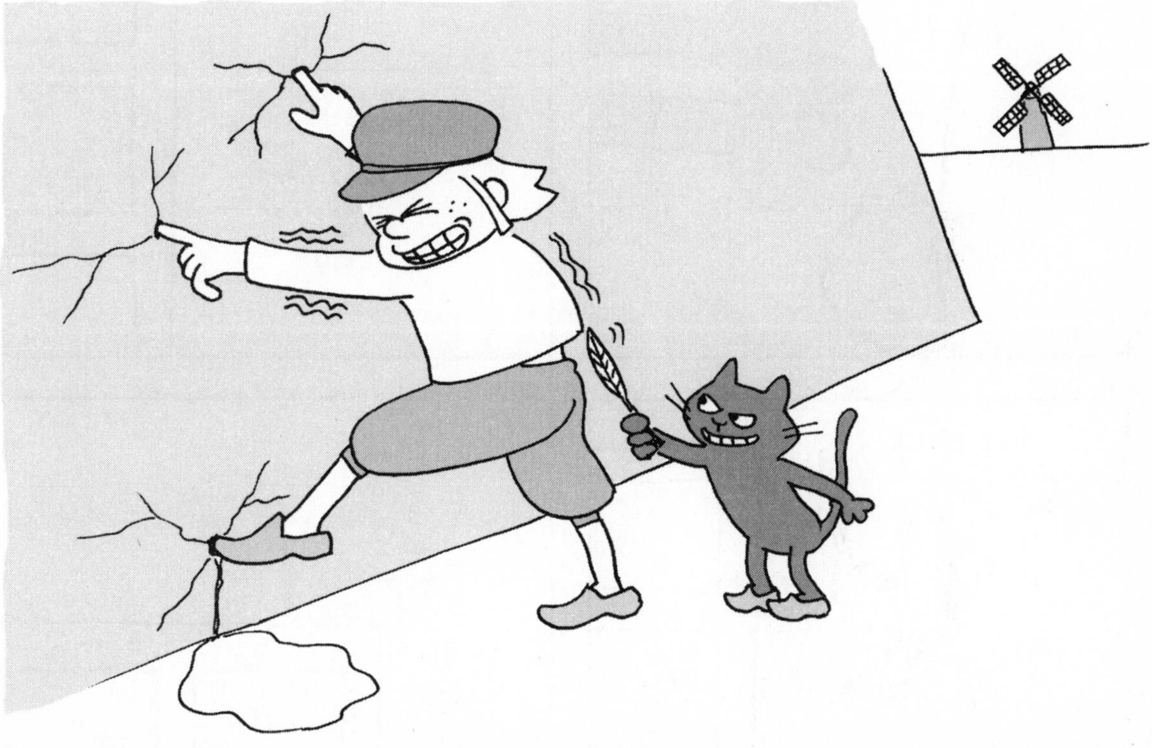

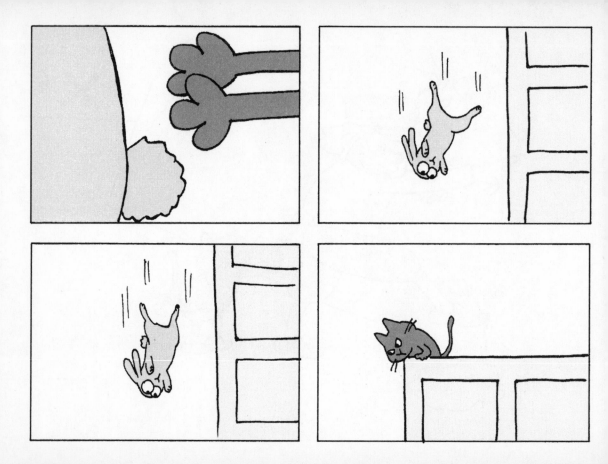

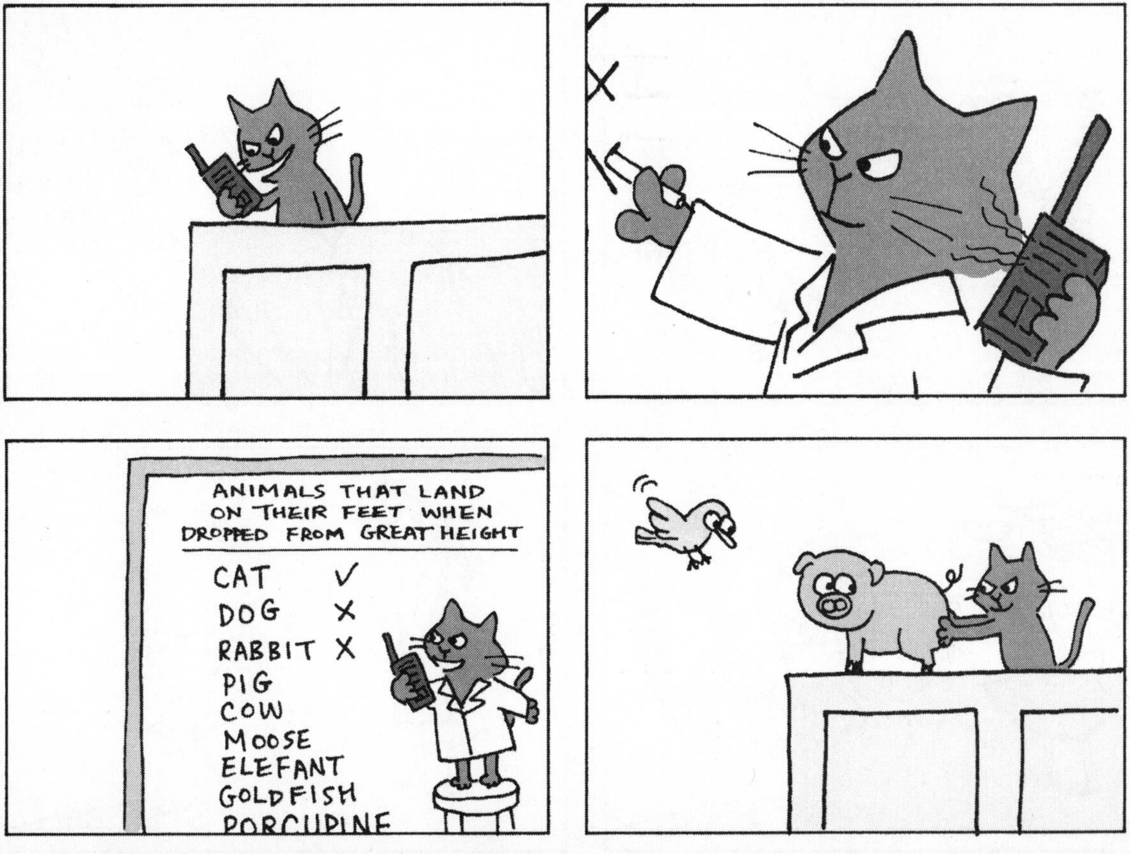
ANIMALS THAT LAND ON THEIR FEET WHEN DROPPED FROM GREAT HEIGHT
CAT ✓
DOG X
RABBIT X
PIG
COW
MOOSE
ELEFANT
GOLDFISH
PORCUPINE

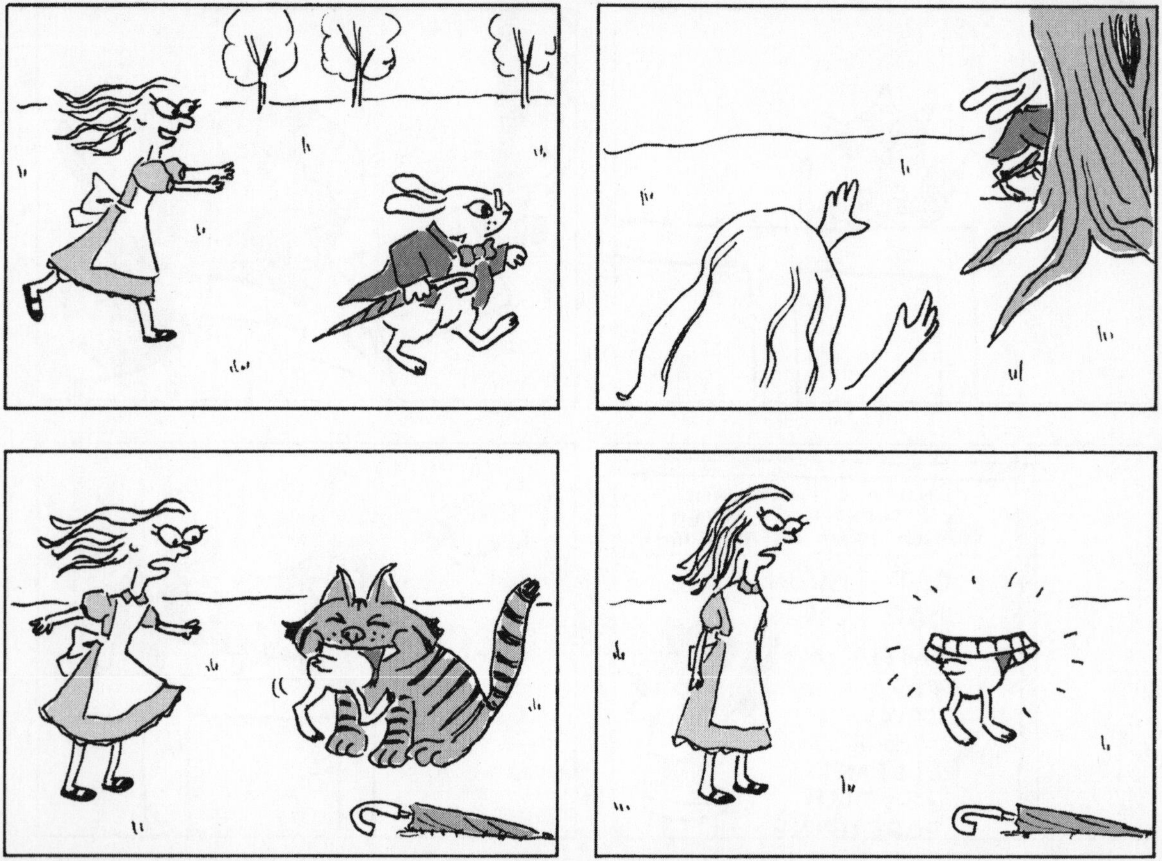

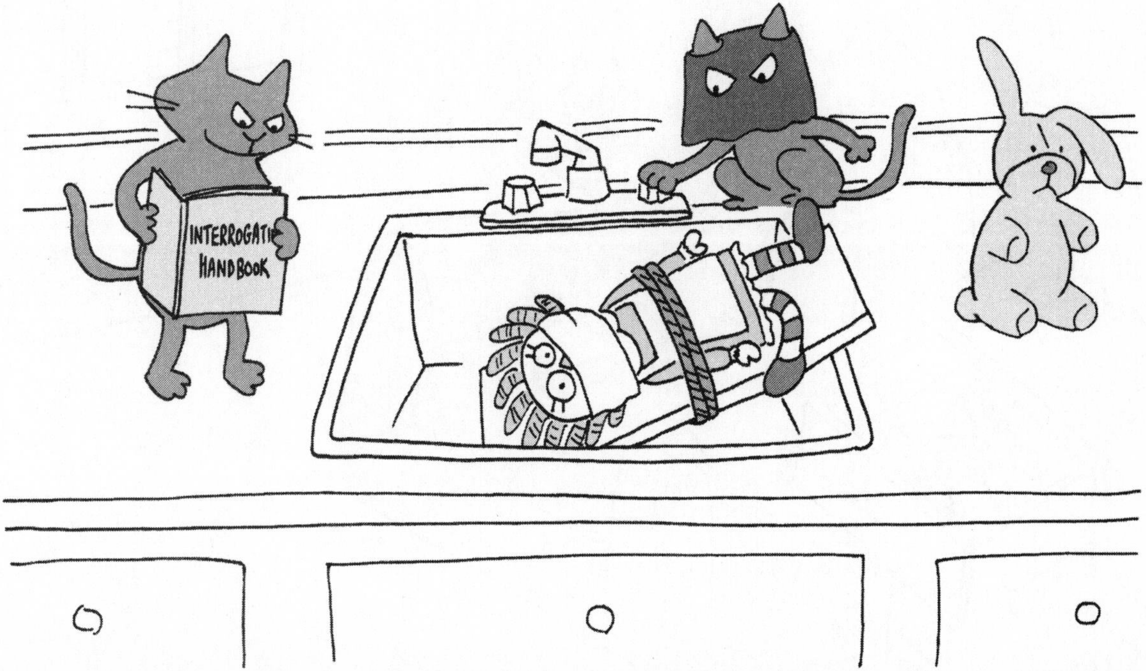
INTERROGATI
HANDBOOK

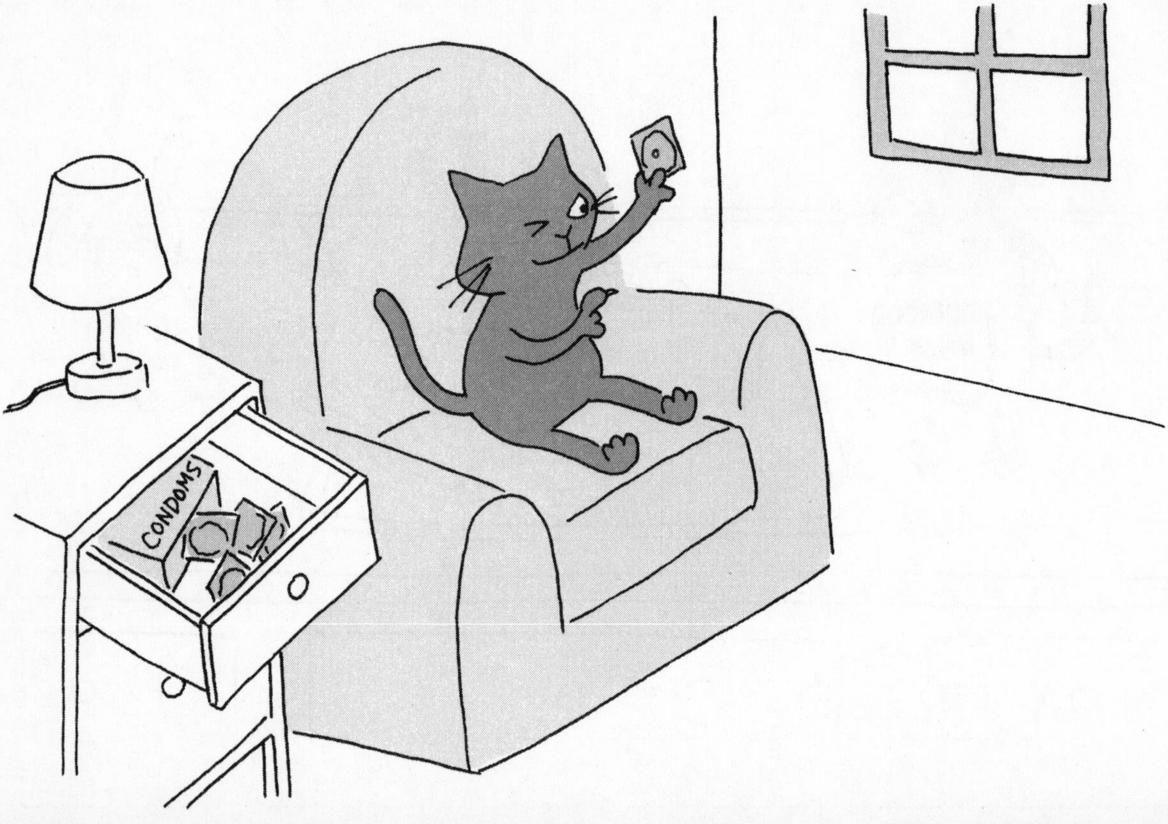
CONDOMS

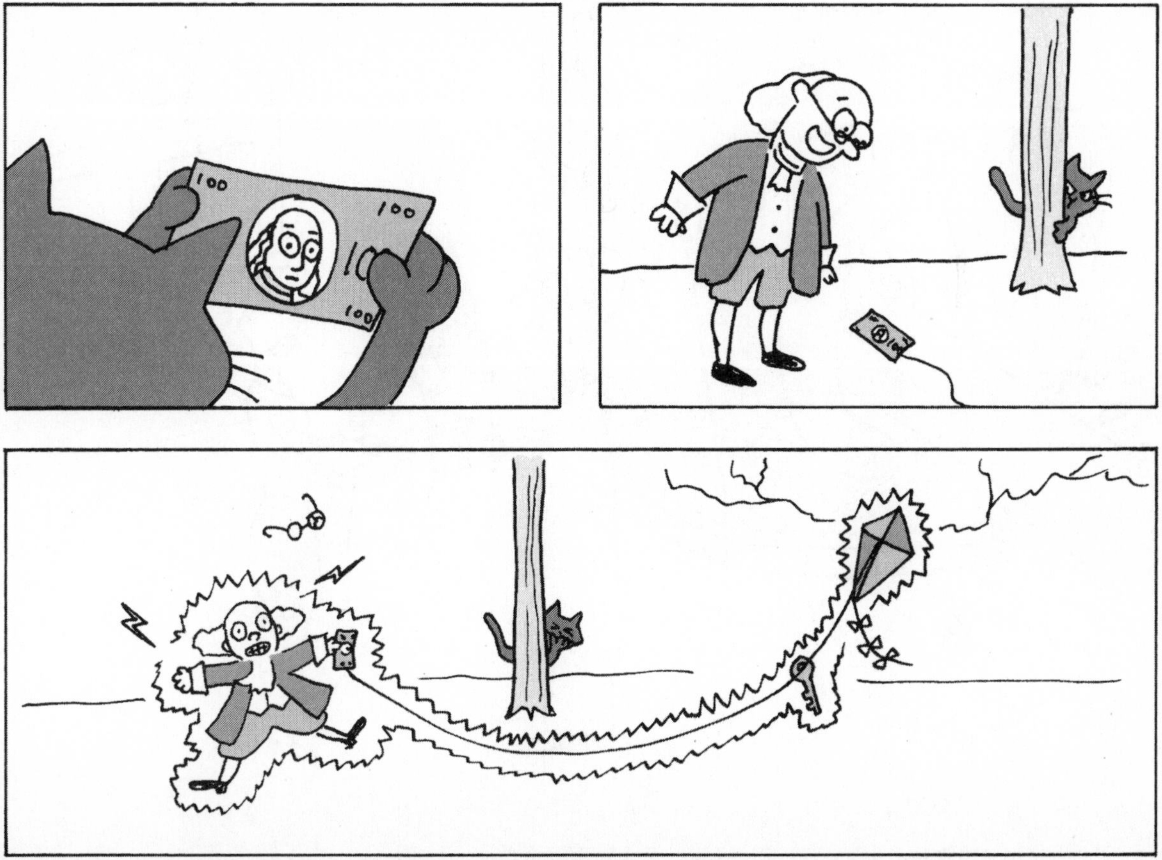
100
100
100

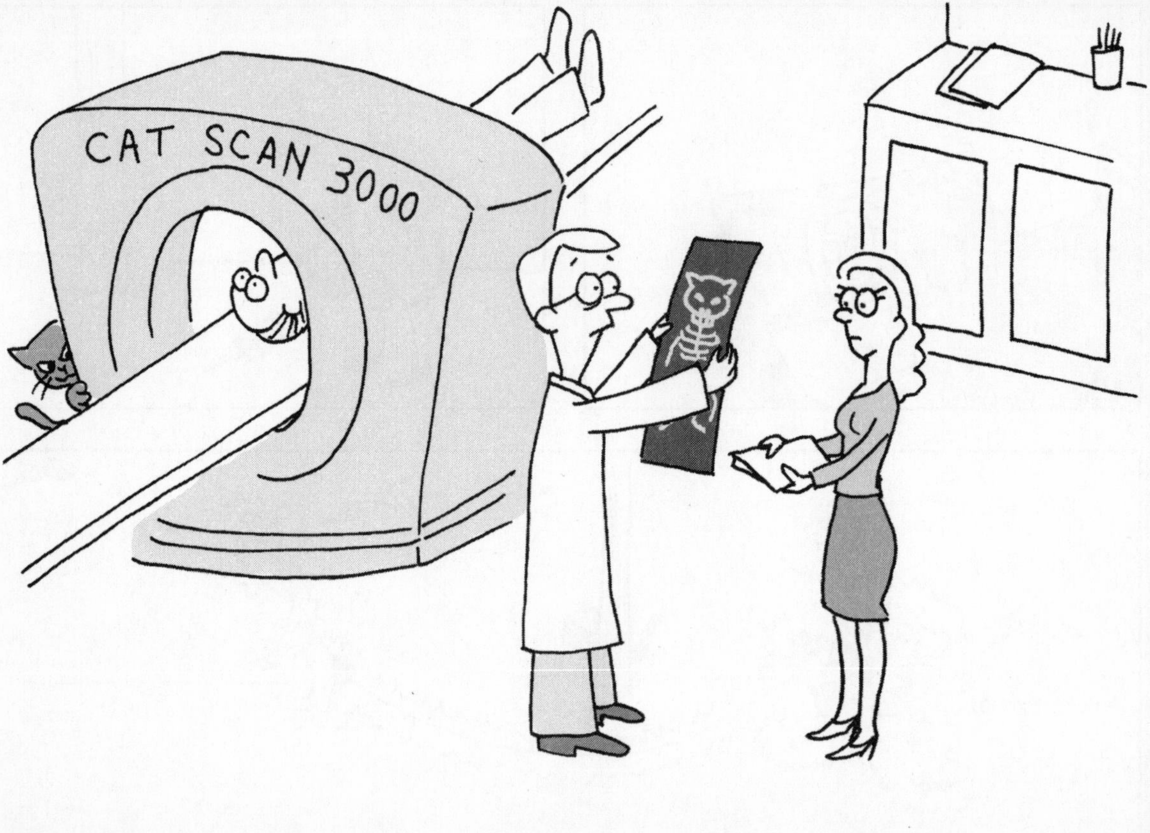
CAT SCAN 3000

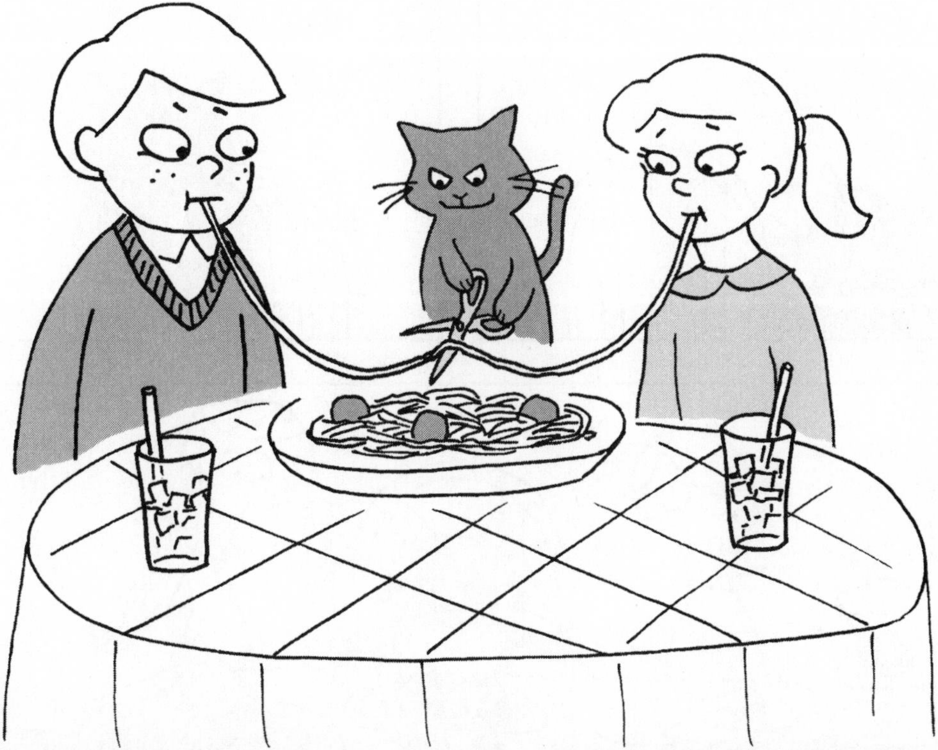

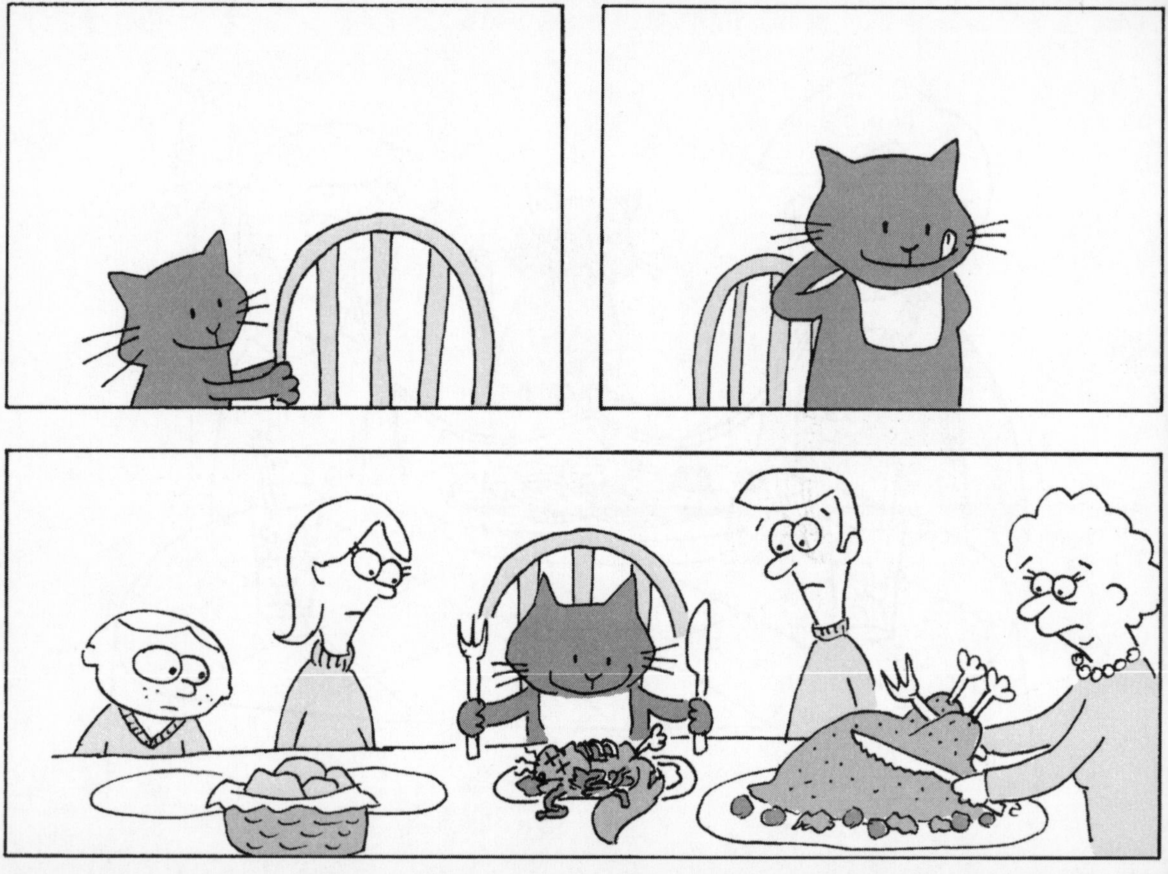

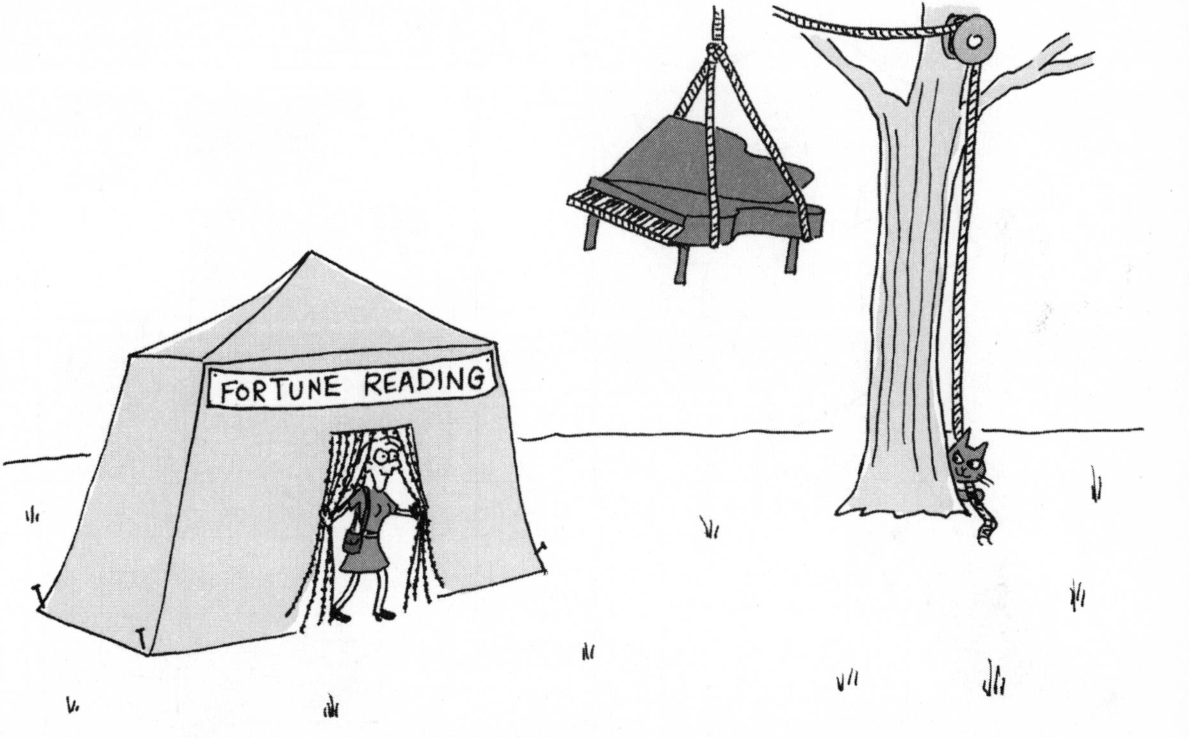
FORTUNE READING

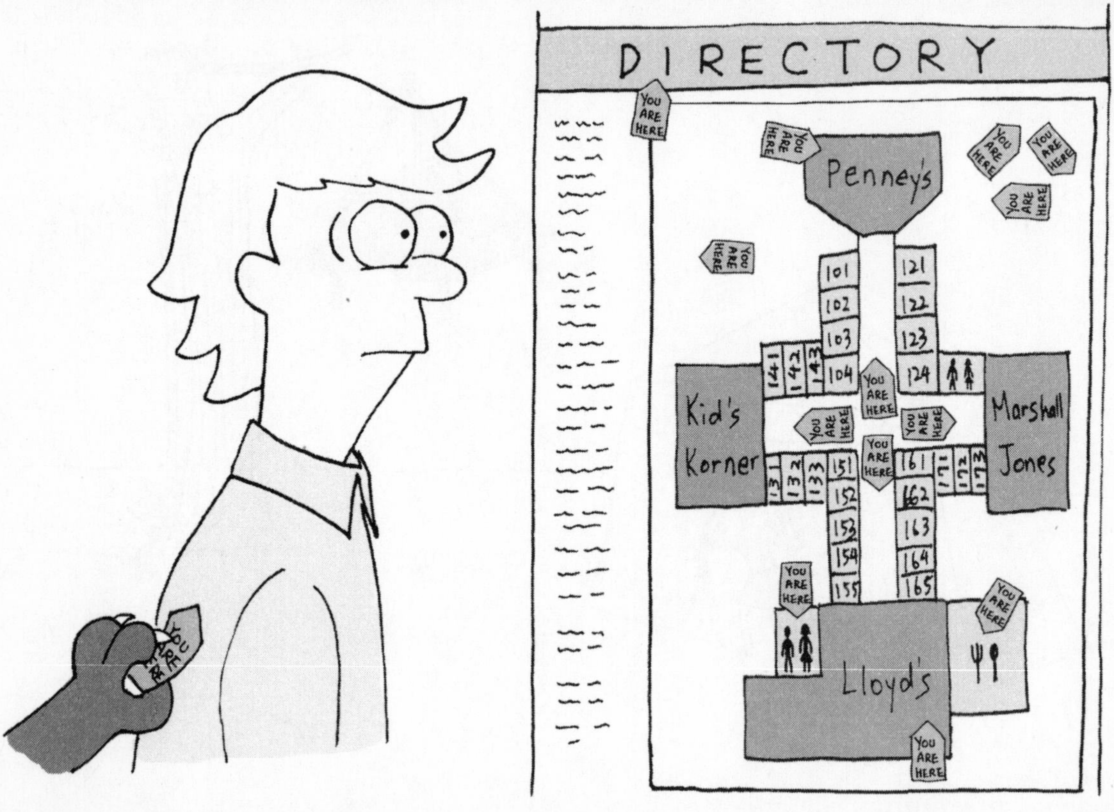

DIRECTORY
Penney's
Kid's Korner
Marshall Jones
Lloyd's
101
102
103
104
121
122
123
124
141
142
143
131
132
133
151
152
153
154
155
161
162
163
164
165
171
172
173
YOU ARE HERE

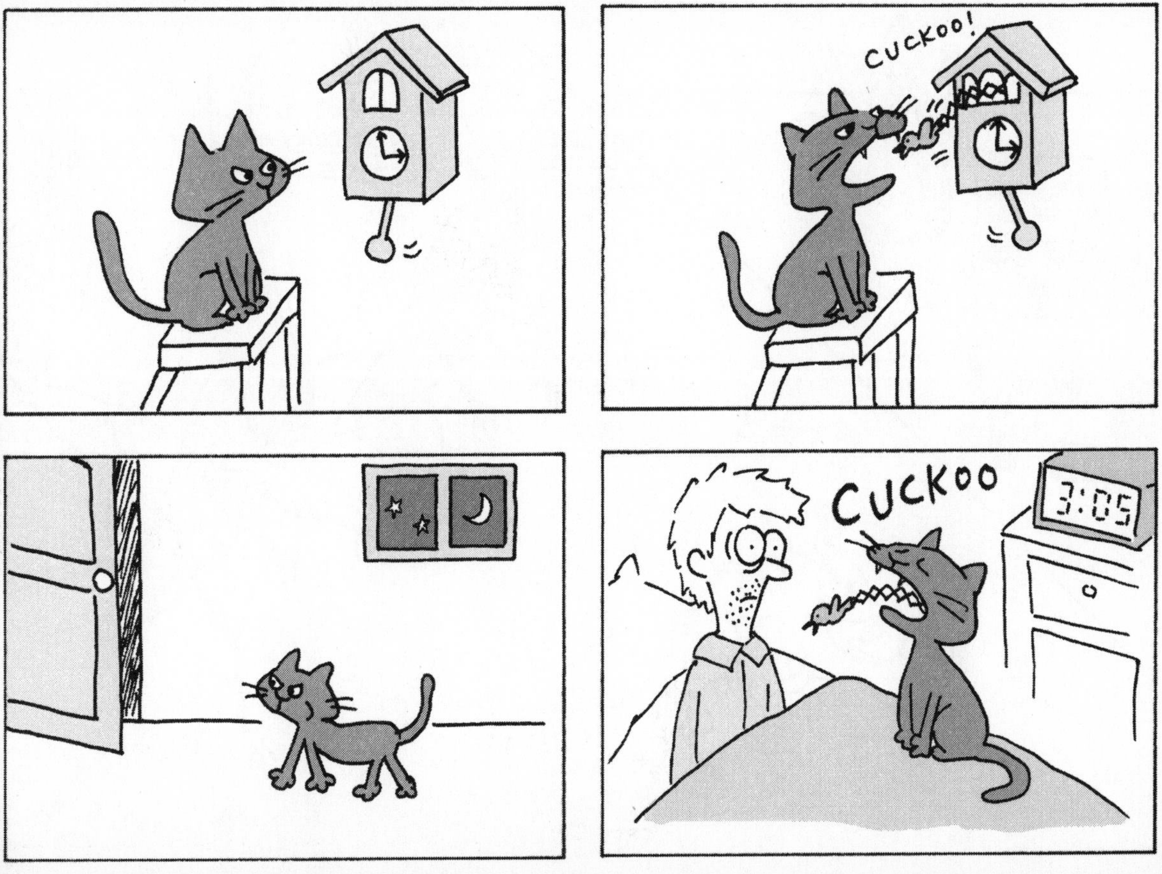
CUCKOO!
CUCKOO
3:05

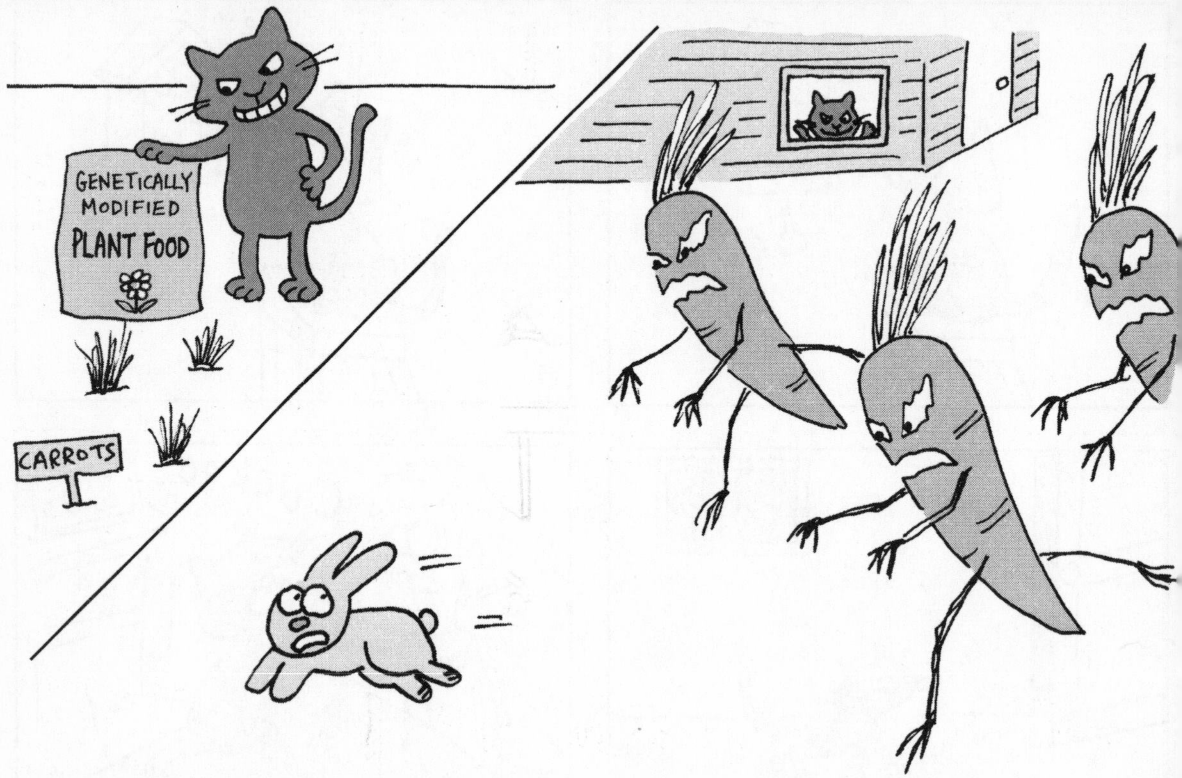
GENETICALLY
MODIFIED
PLANT FOOD
CARROTS

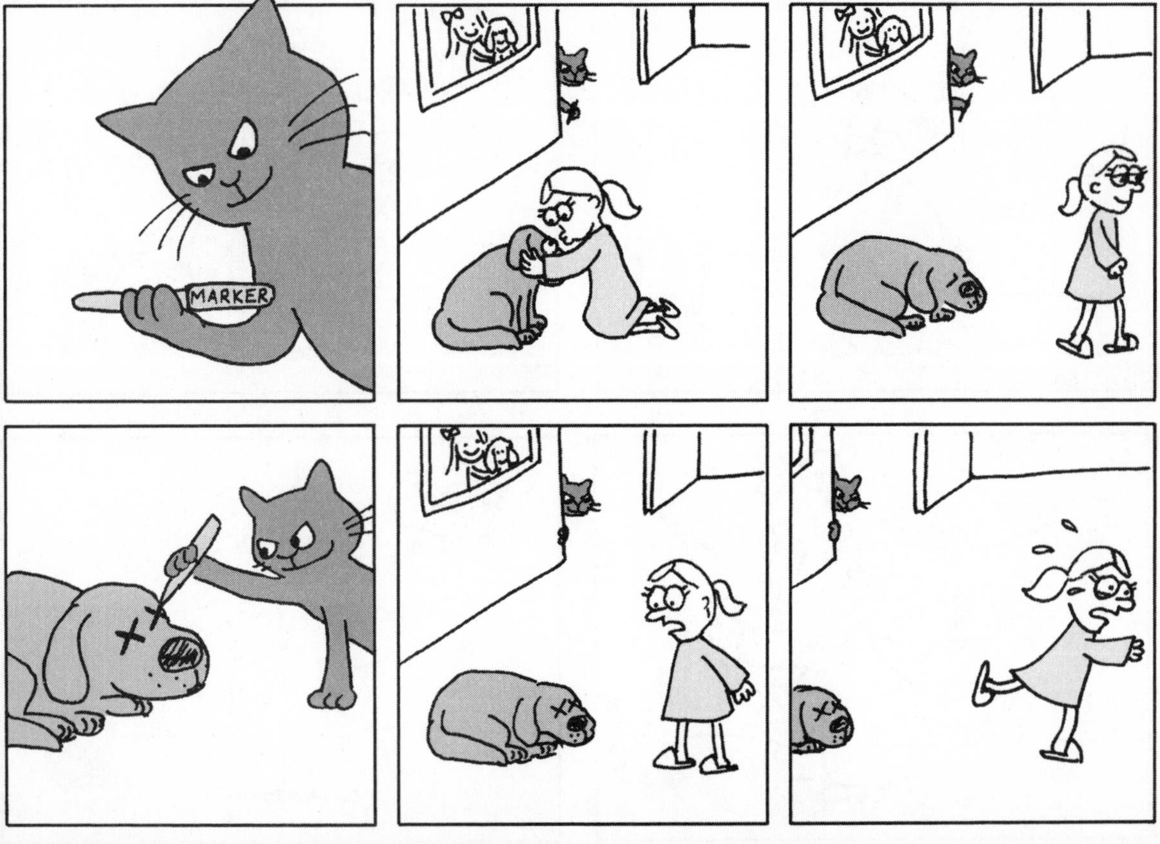
MARKER

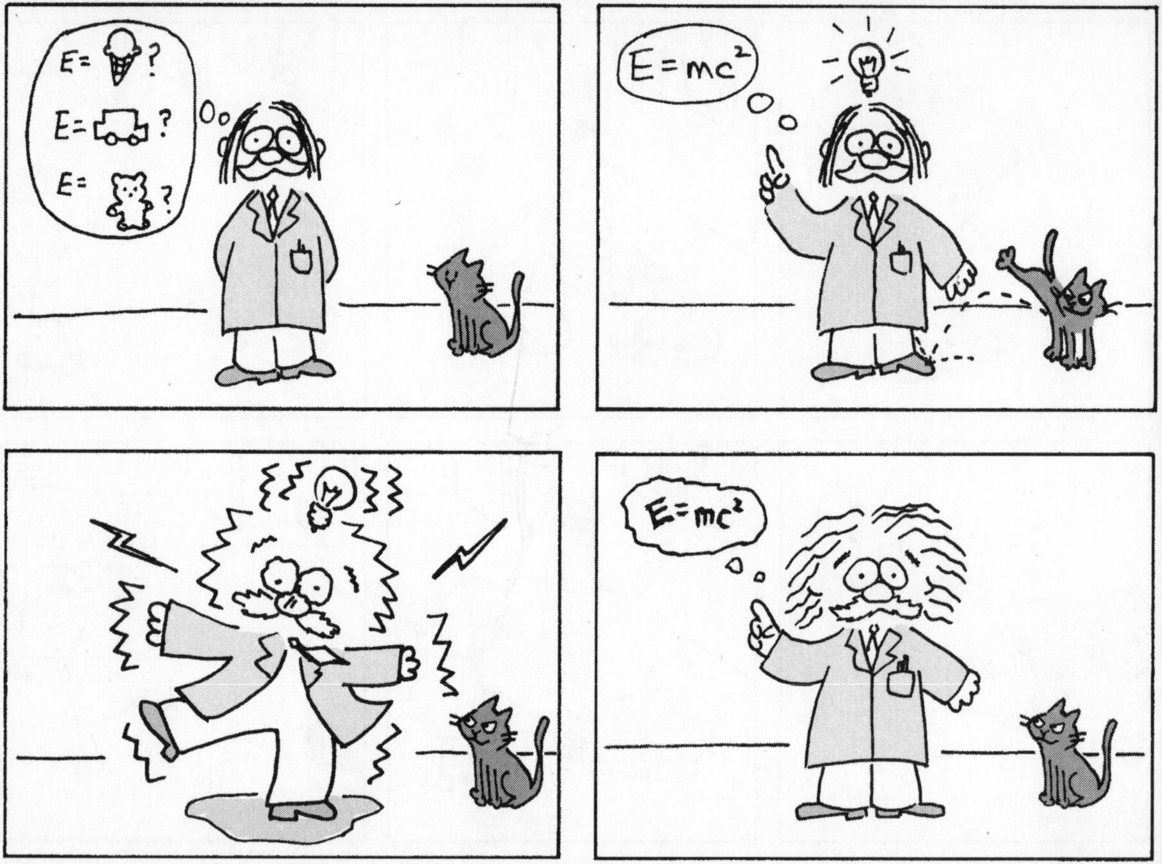
E= ?
E= ?
E= ?
E=mc²
E=mc²

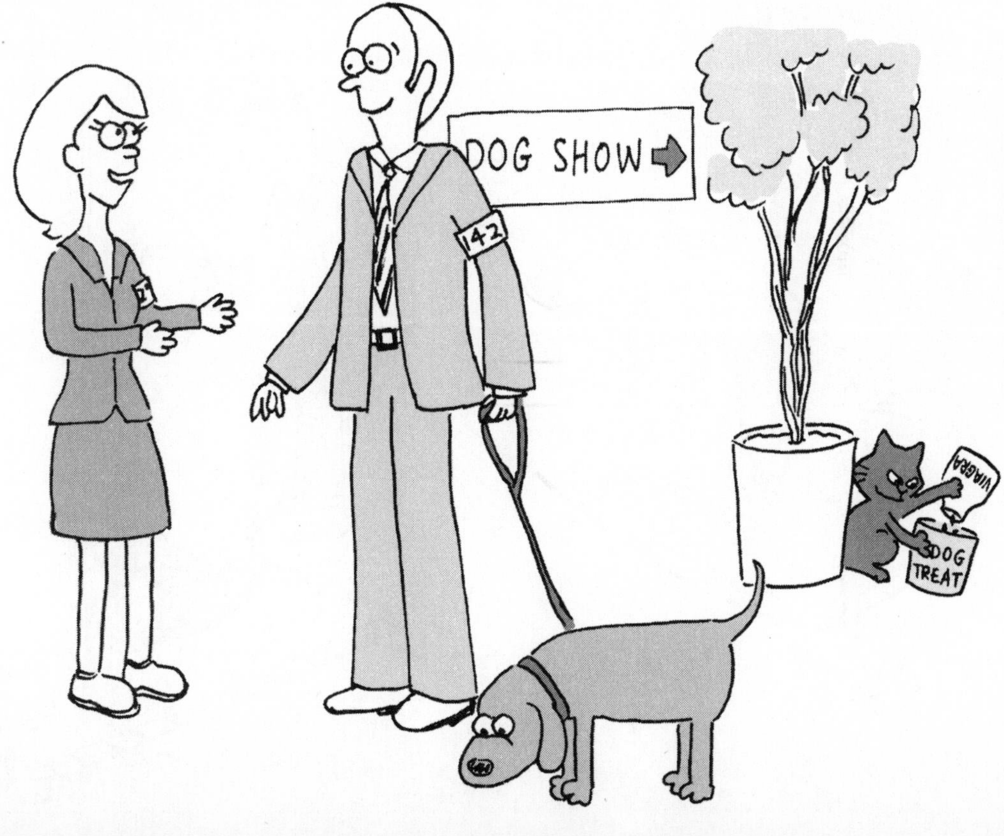
DOG SHOW
142
VIAGRA
DOG
TREAT

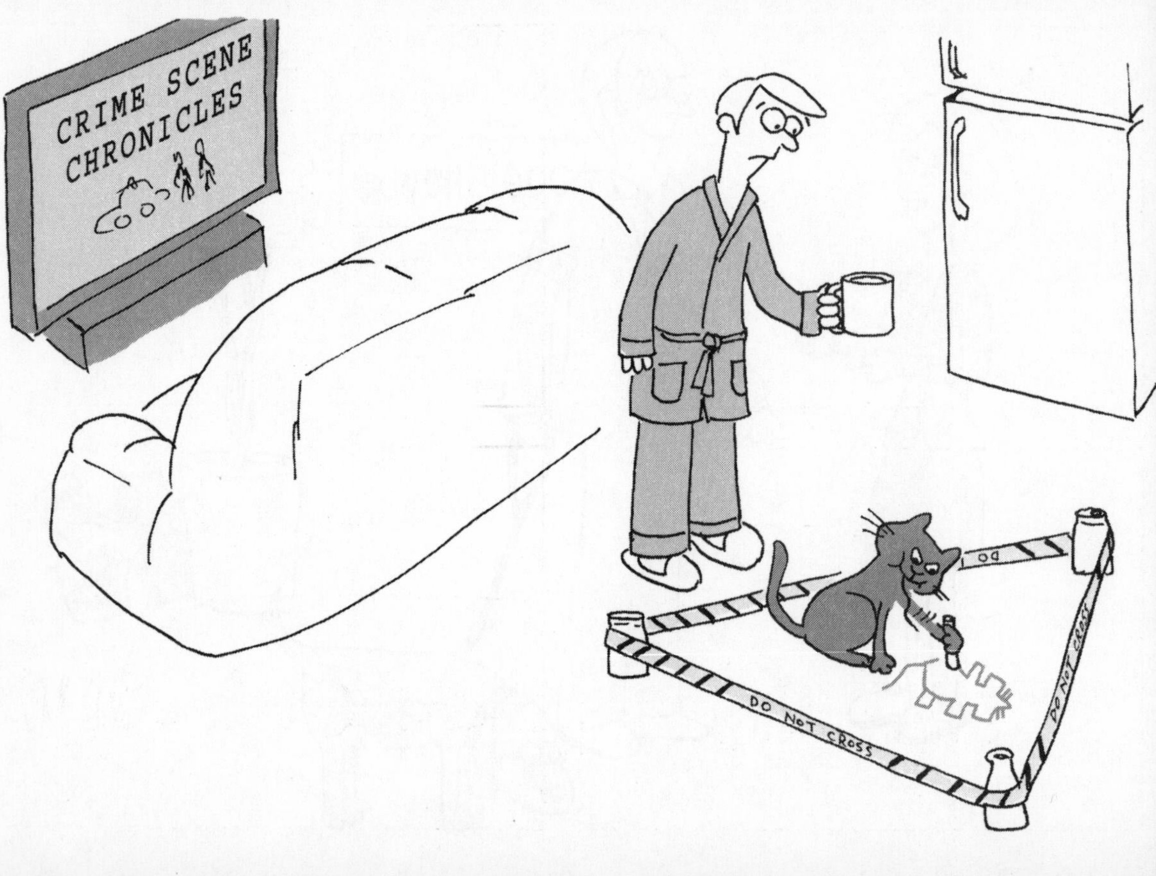
CRIME SCENE
CHRONICLES
DO NOT CROSS
DO NOT CROSS

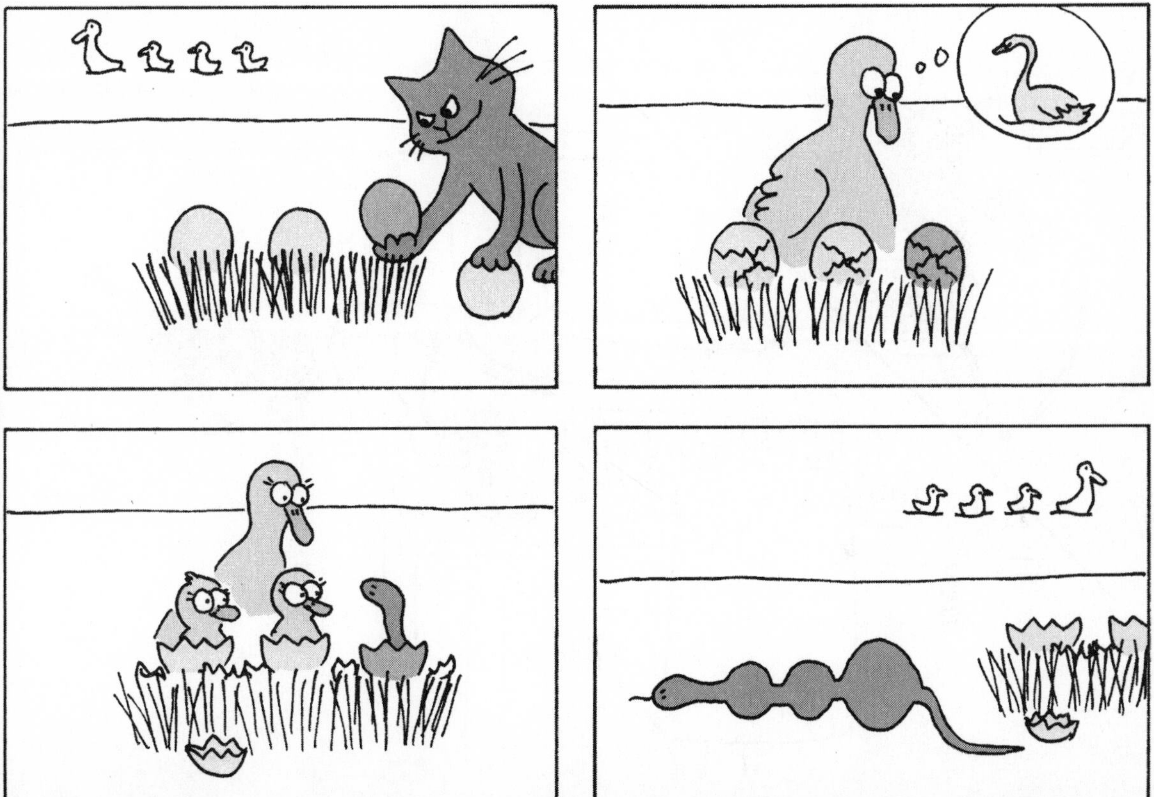

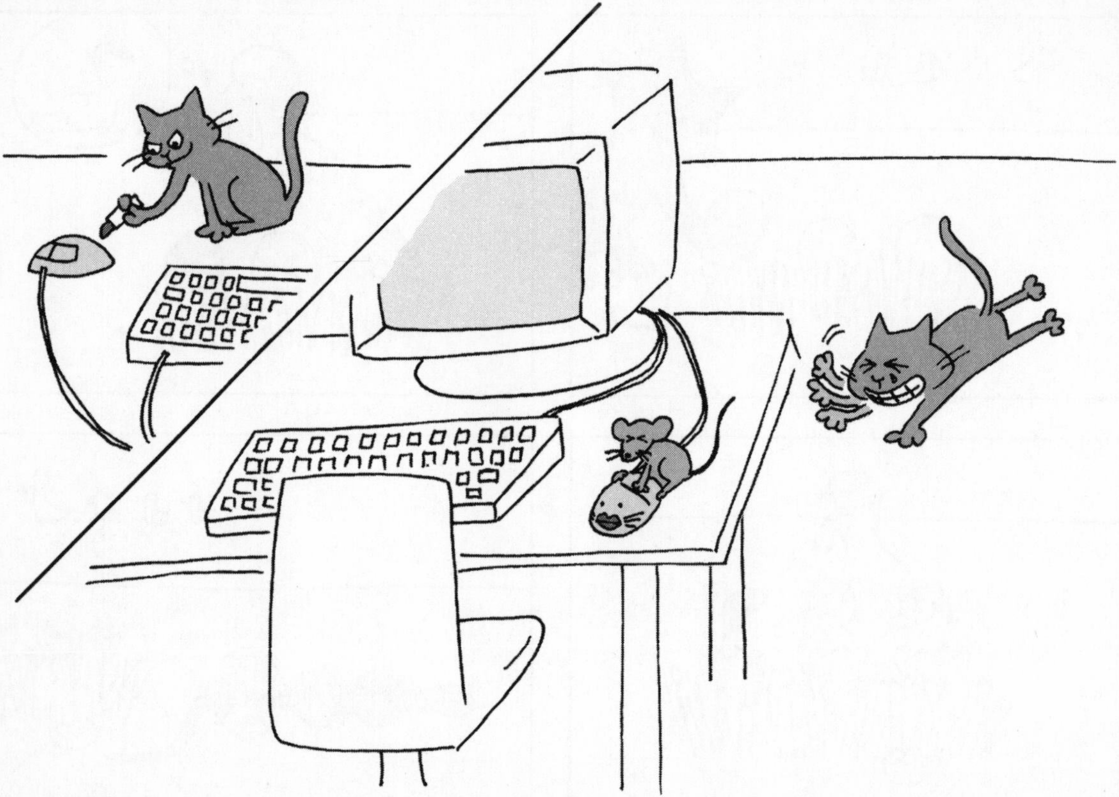

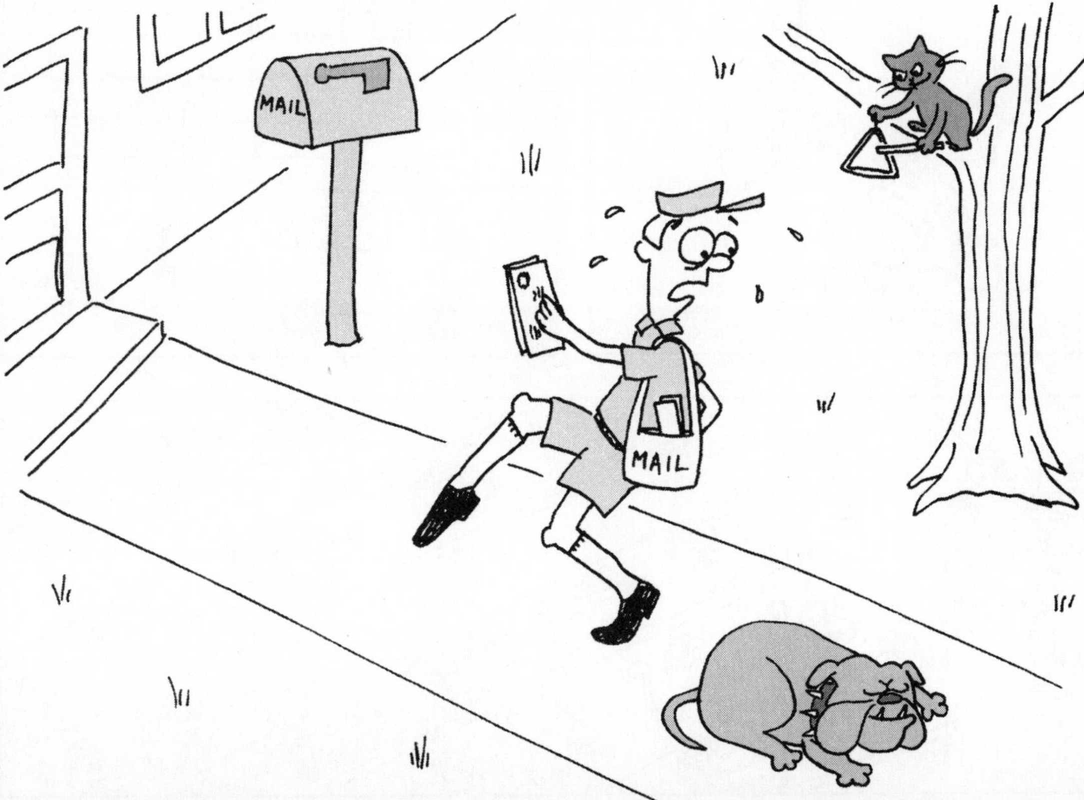

MAIL
MAIL

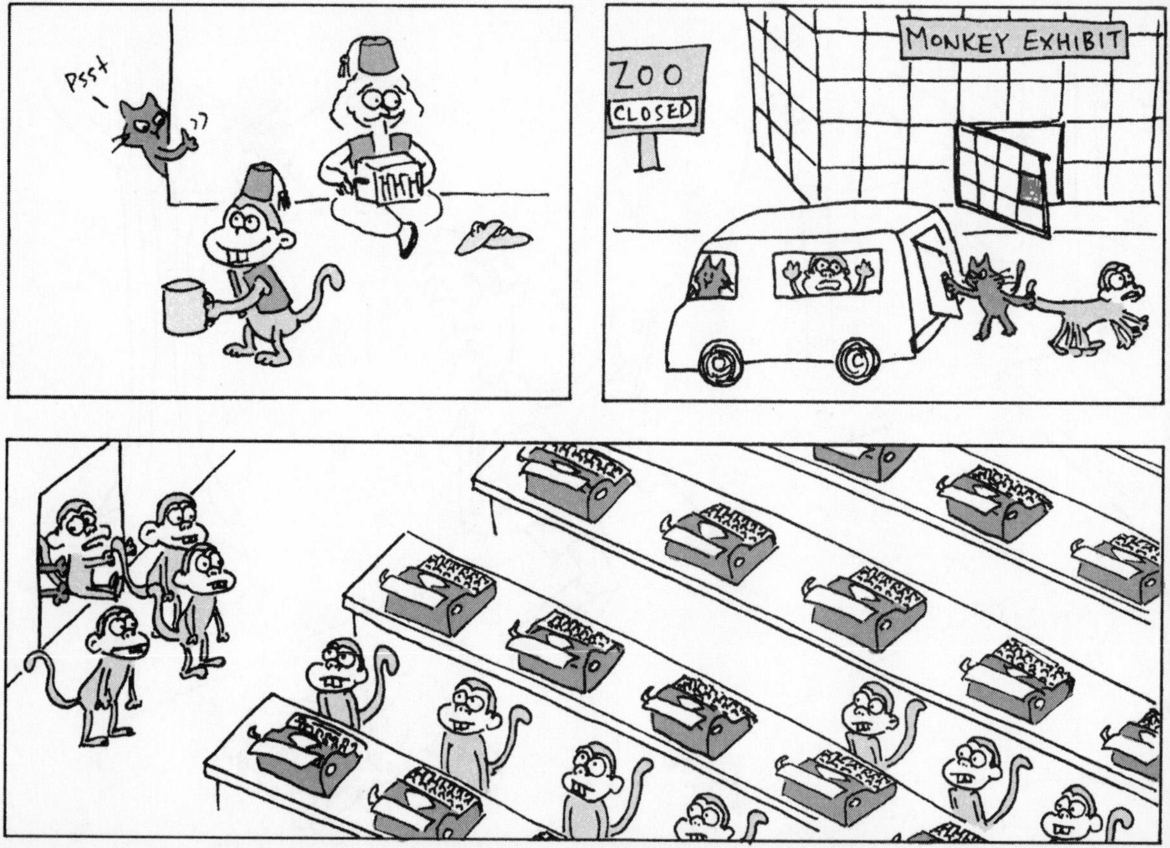
Psst
ZOO
CLOSED
MONKEY EXHIBIT

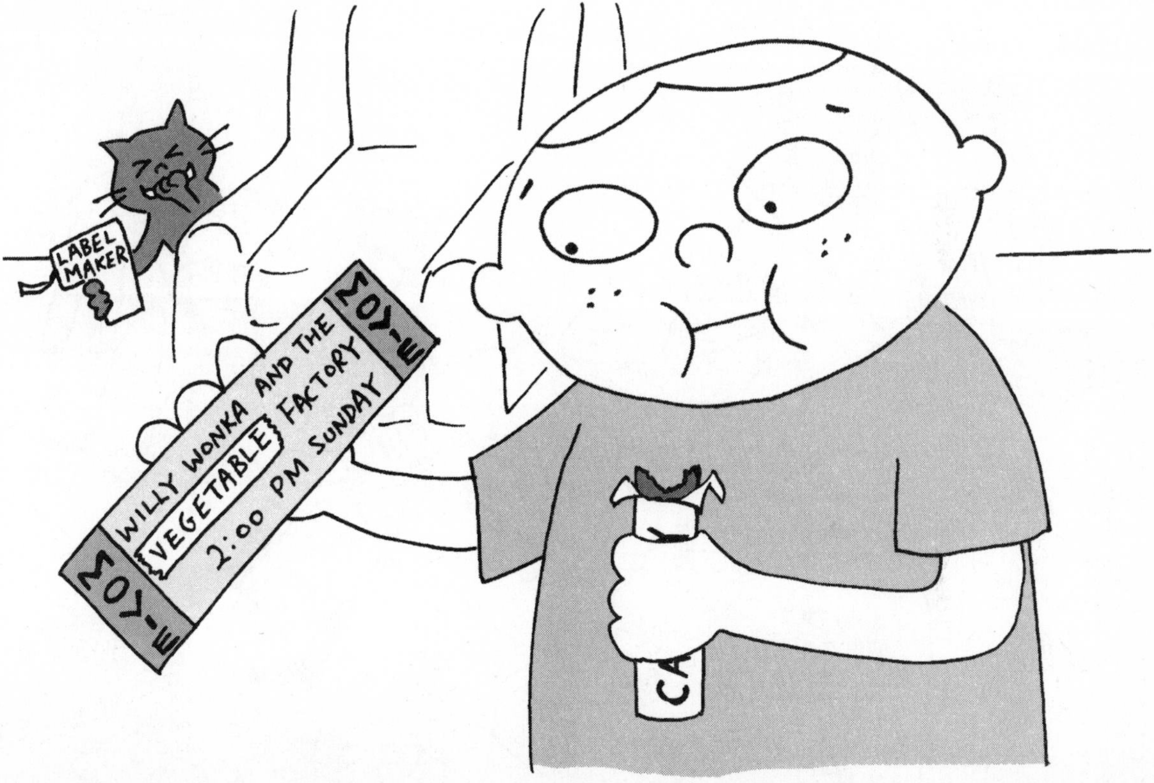
LABEL MAKER
WILLY WONKA AND THE
VEGETABLE FACTORY
2:00 PM SUNDAY

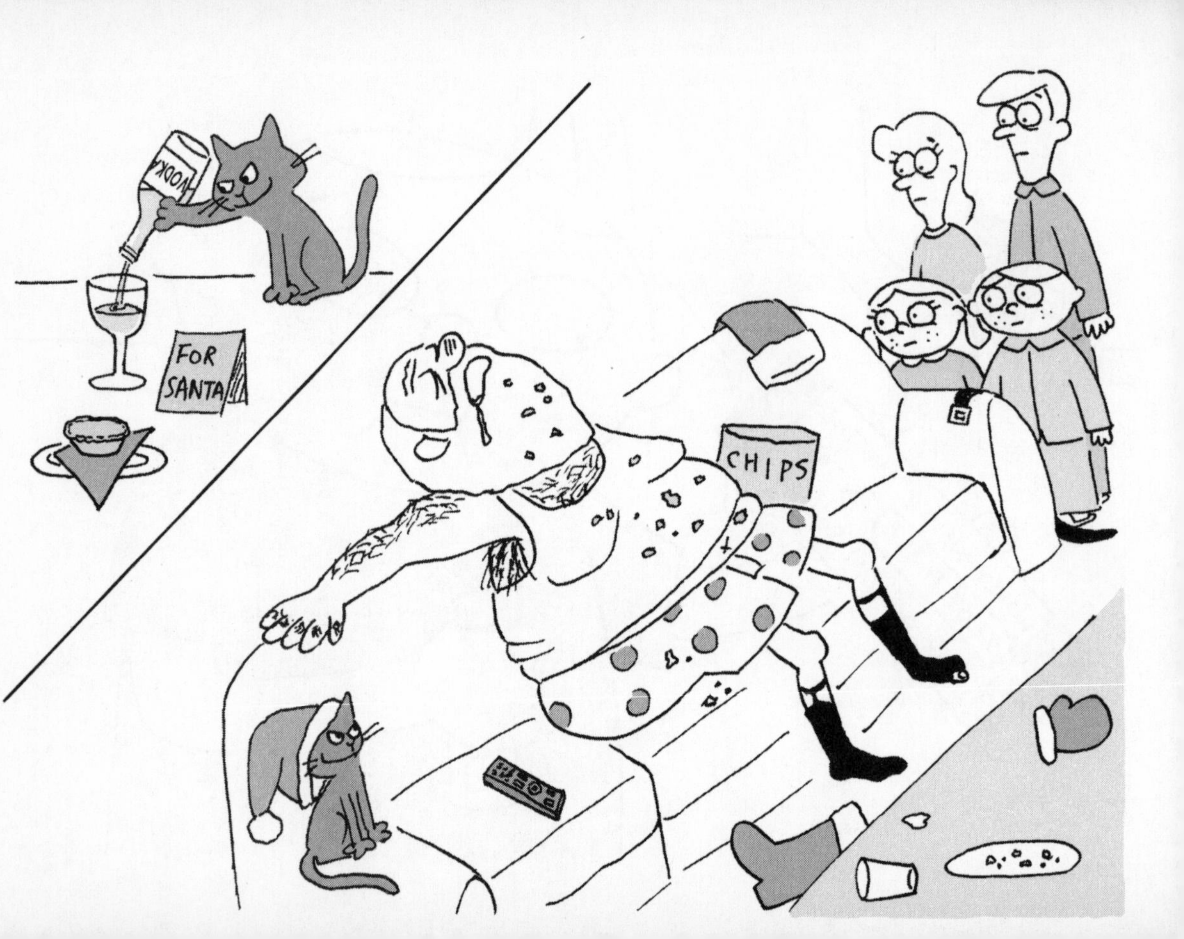
VODKA
FOR SANTA
CHIPS

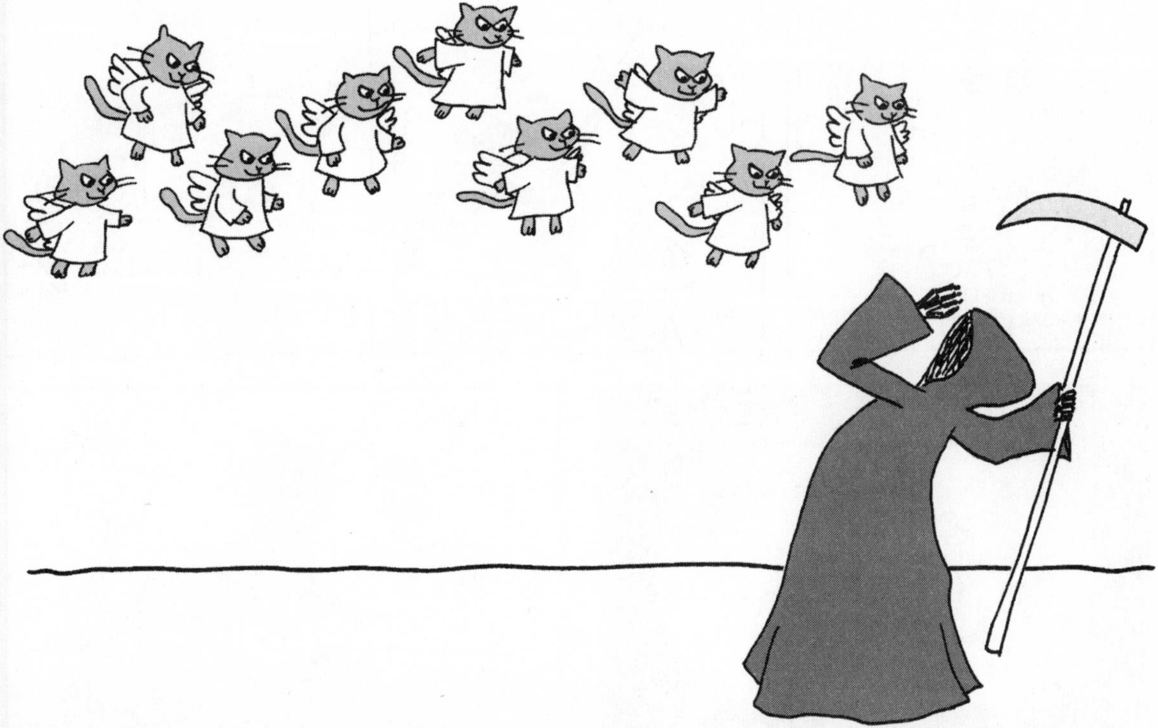

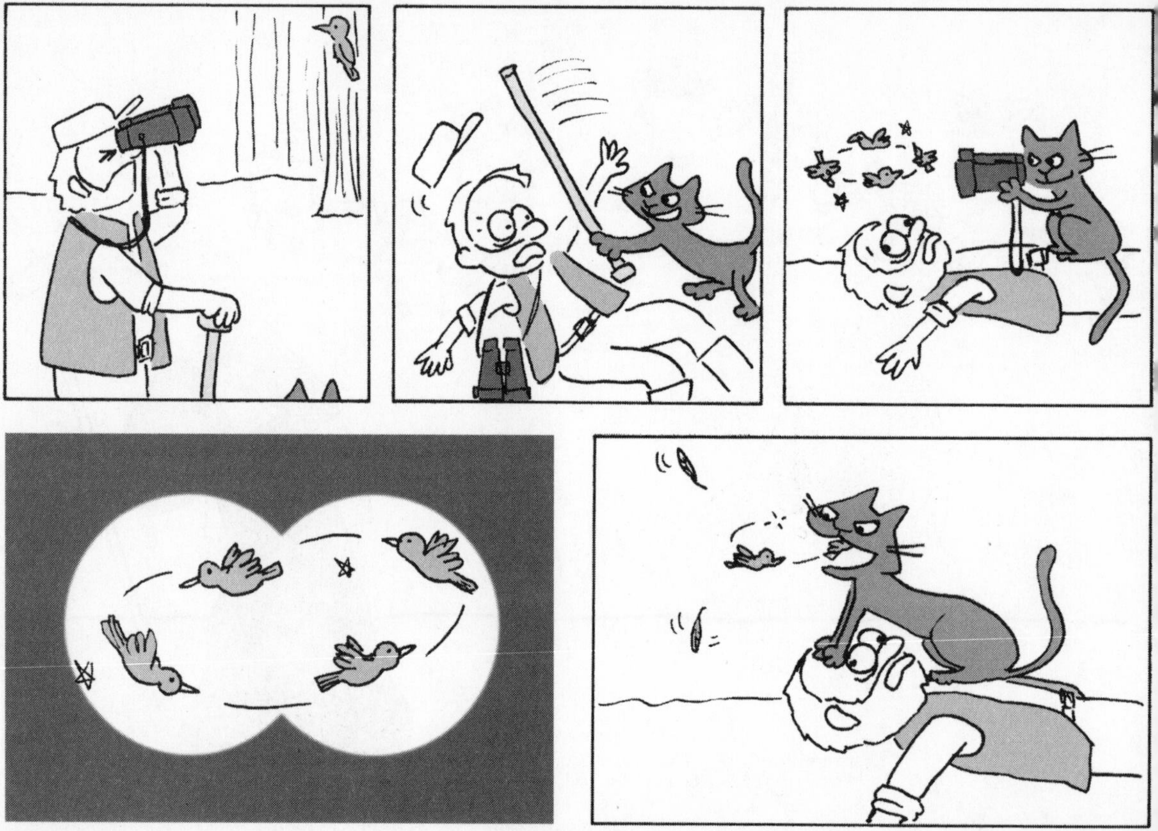

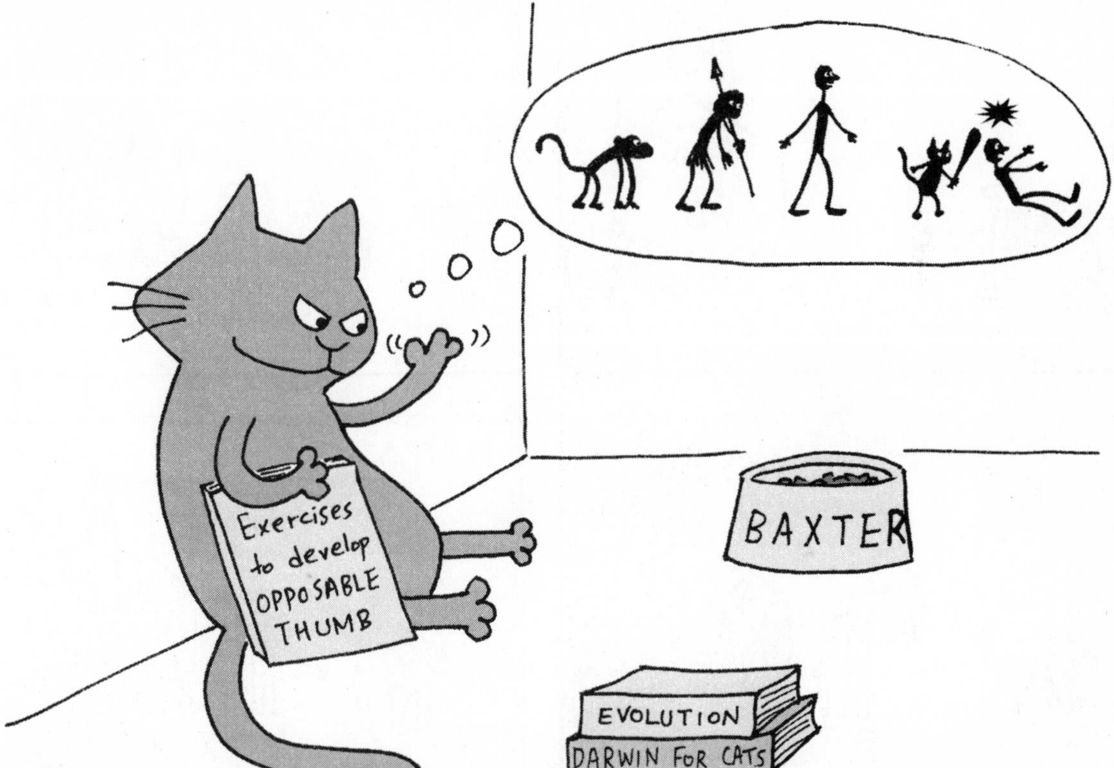
Exercises to develop OPPOSABLE THUMB
BAXTER
EVOLUTION
DARWIN FOR CATS

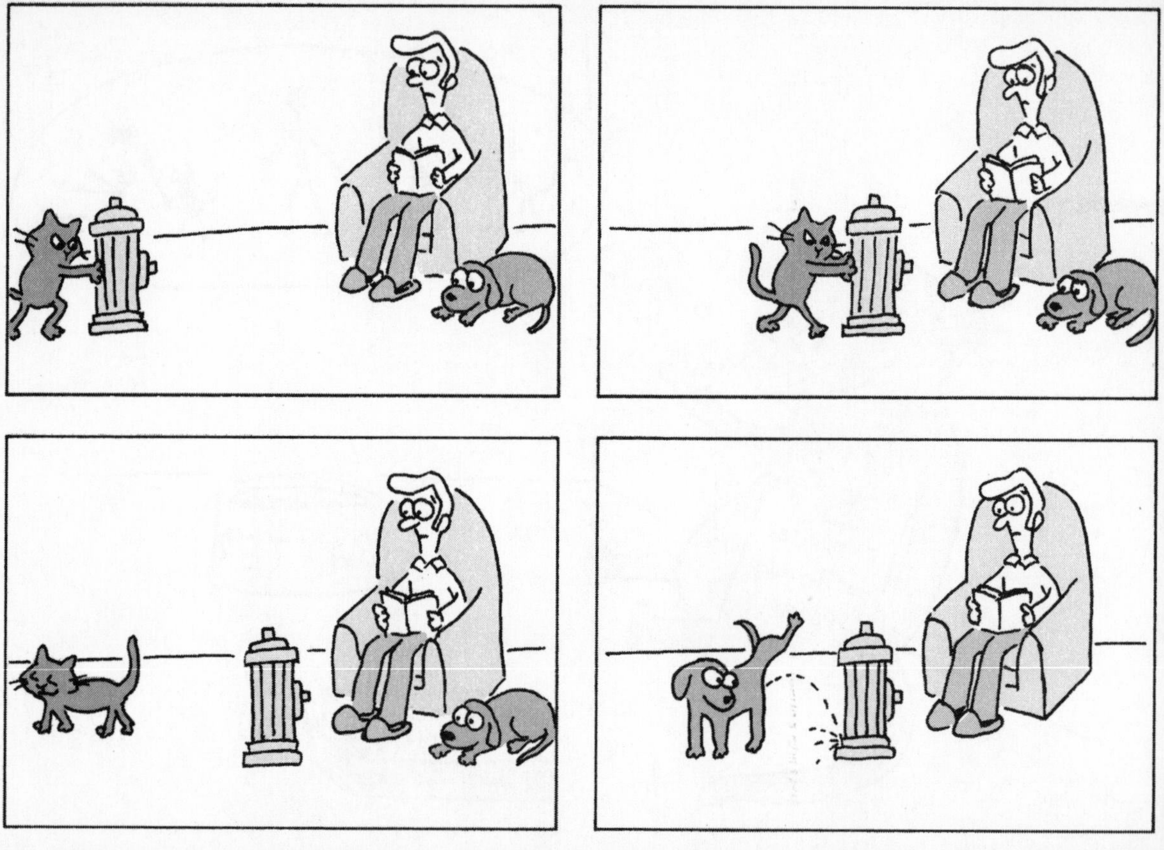

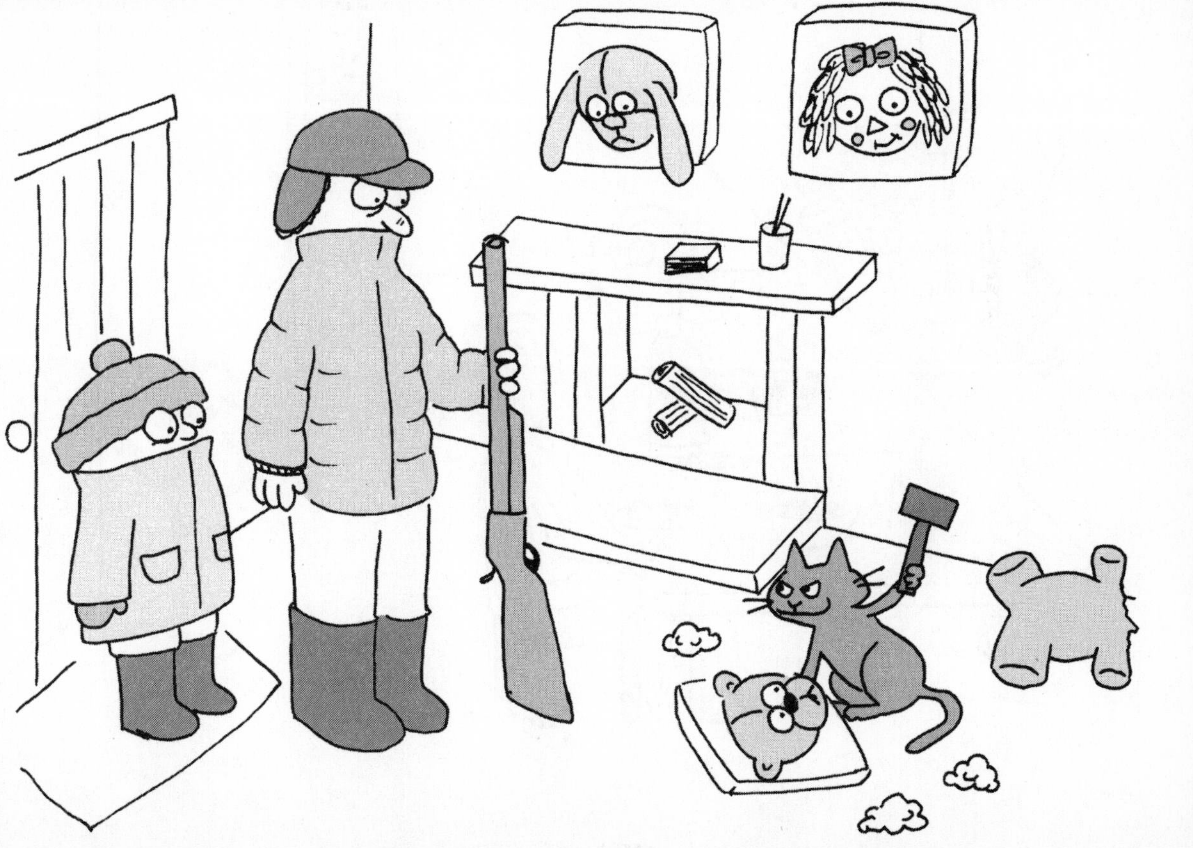

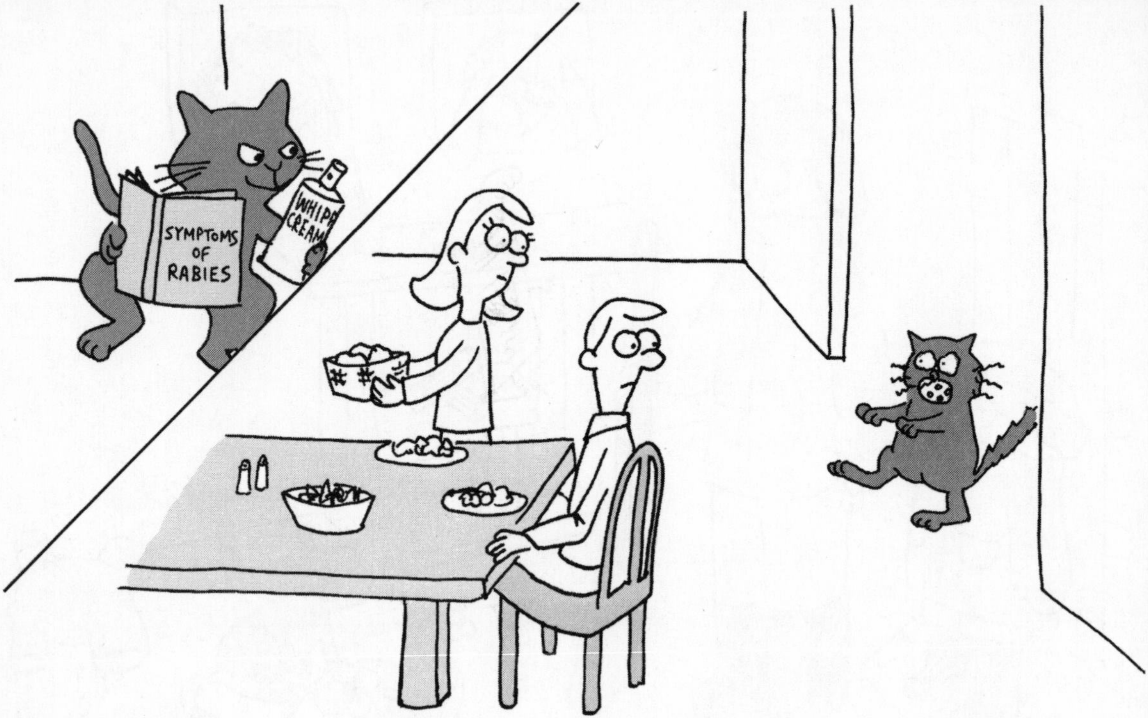
SYMPTOMS OF RABIES
WHIPP CREAM

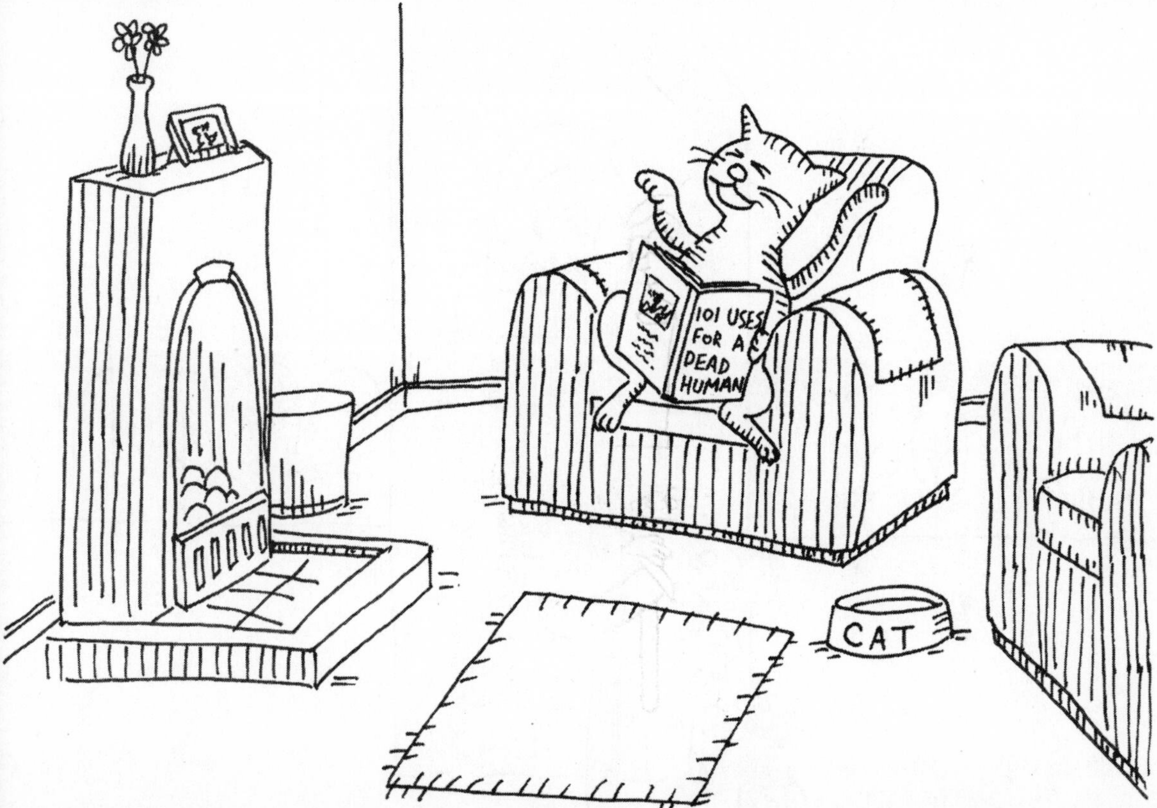
101 USES
FOR A
DEAD
HUMAN
CAT

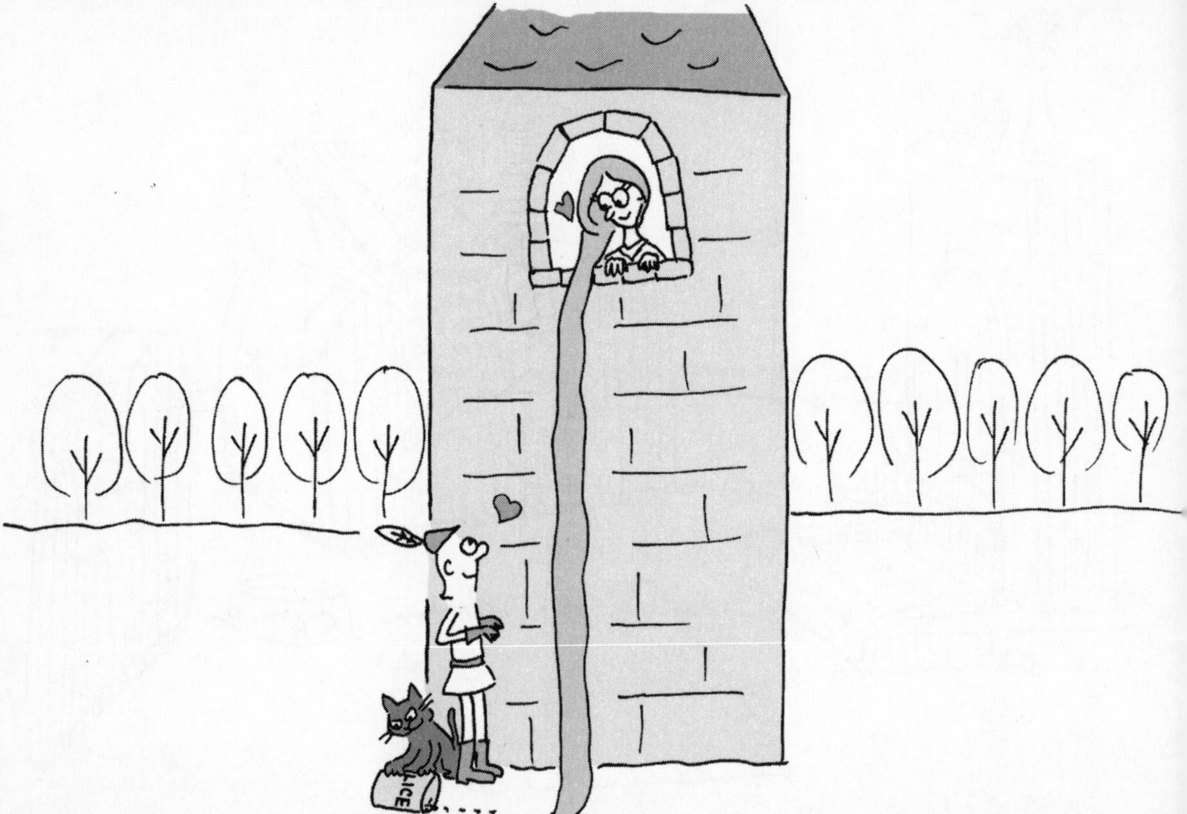

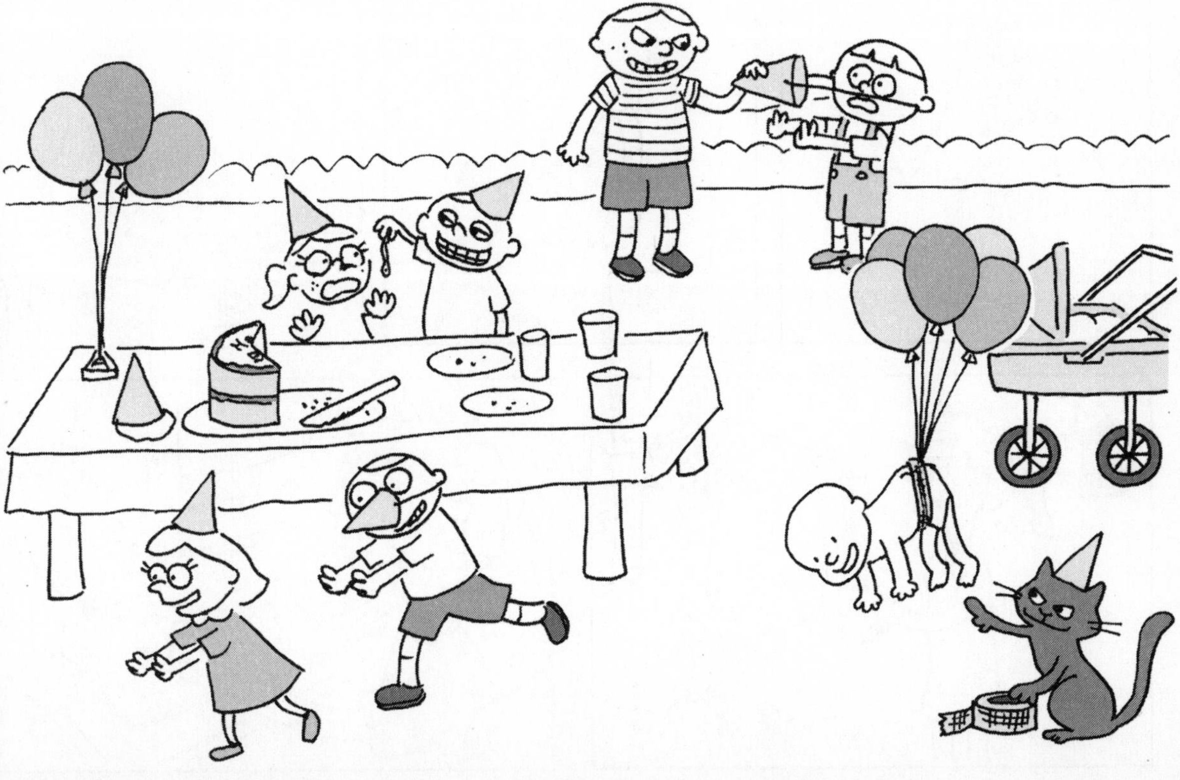

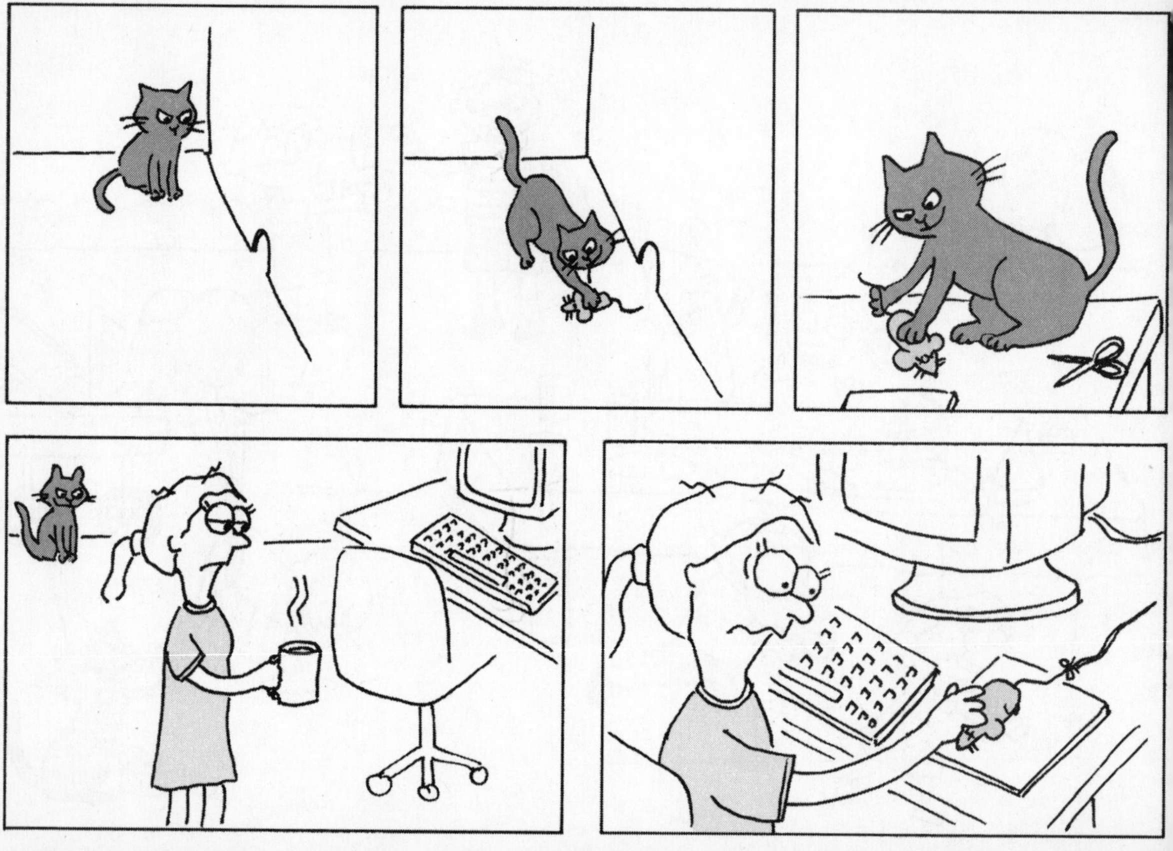

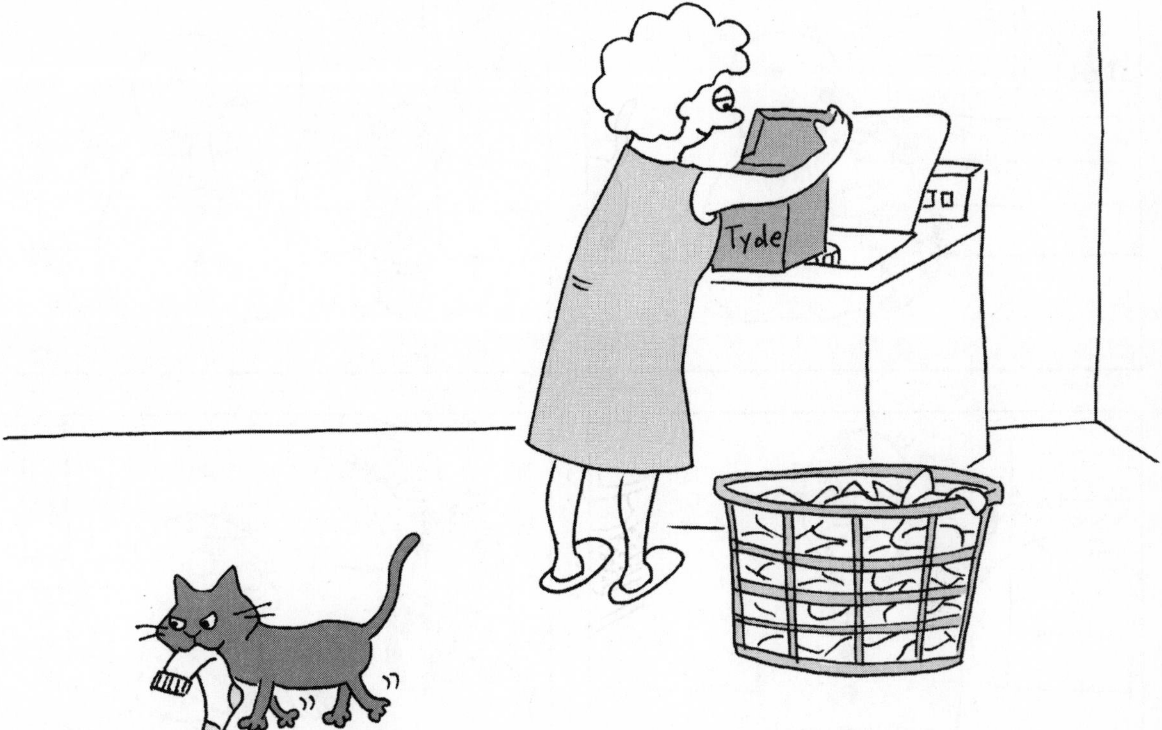
Tyde
JO

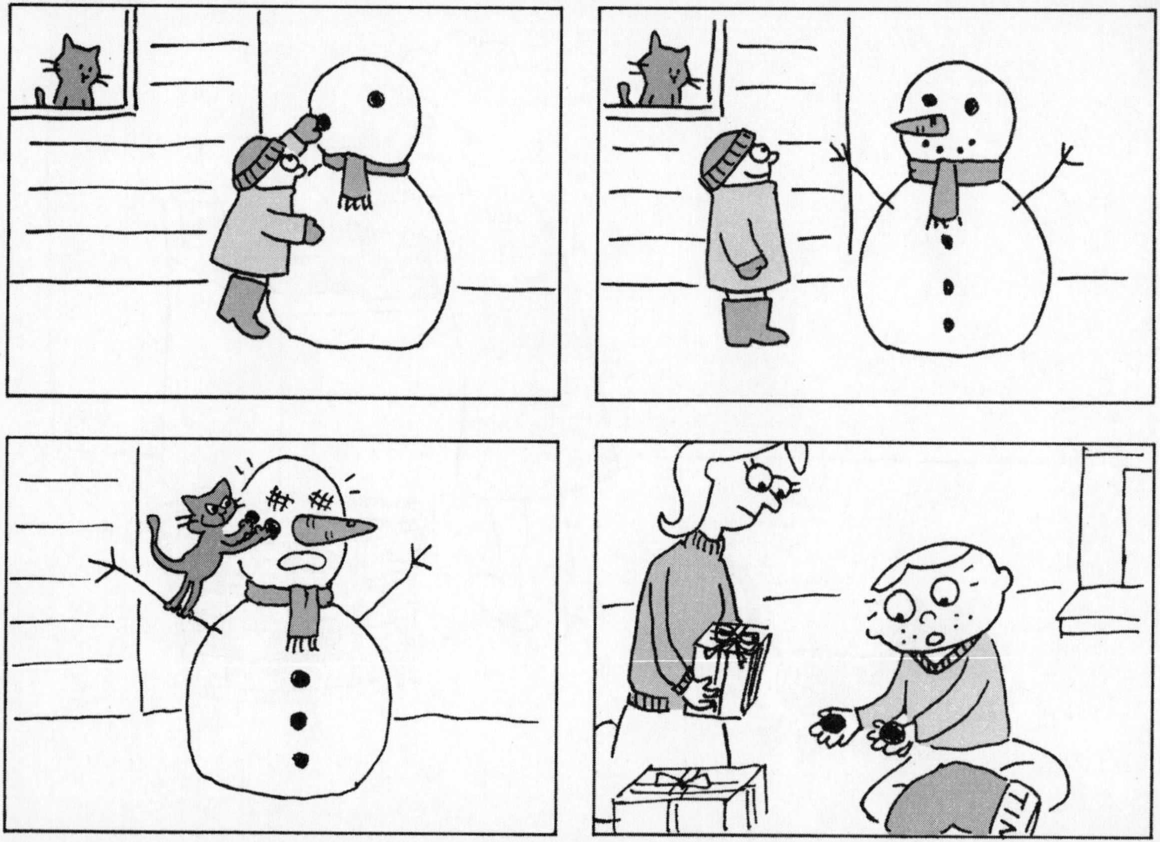

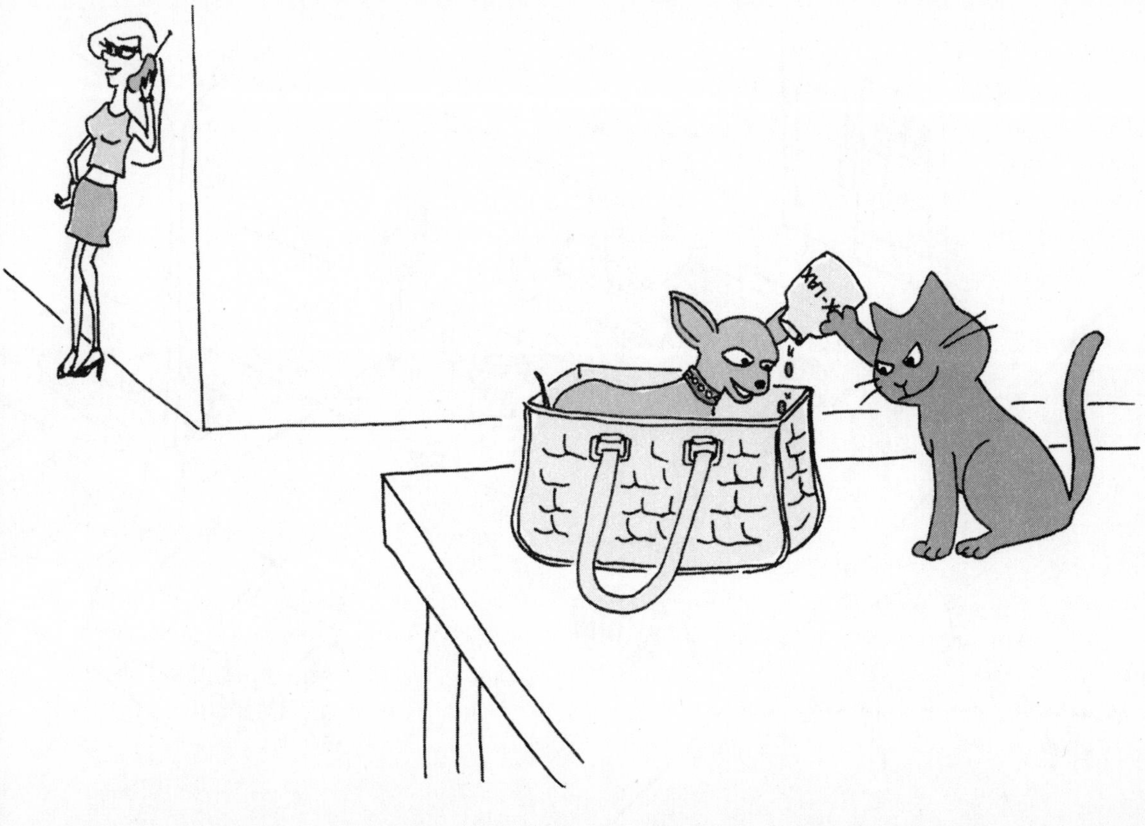
-LAX

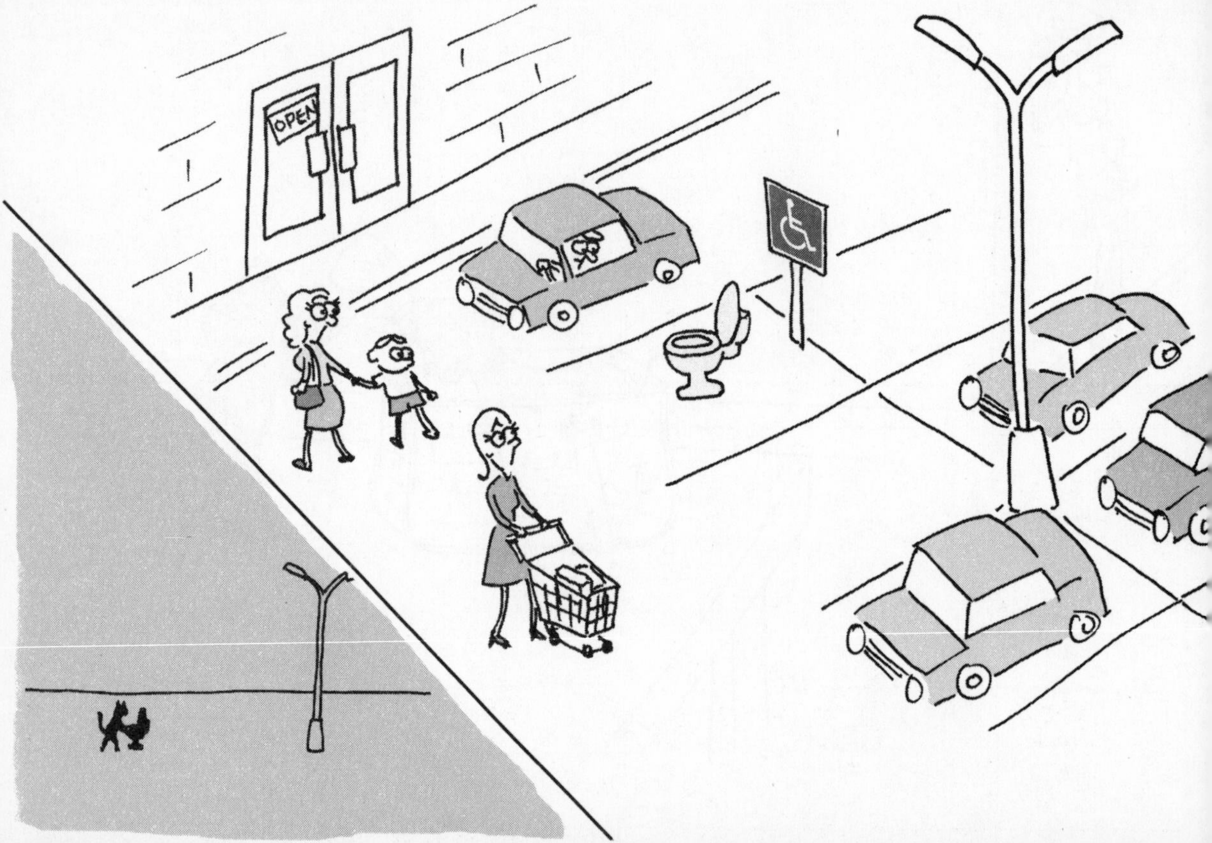
OPEN

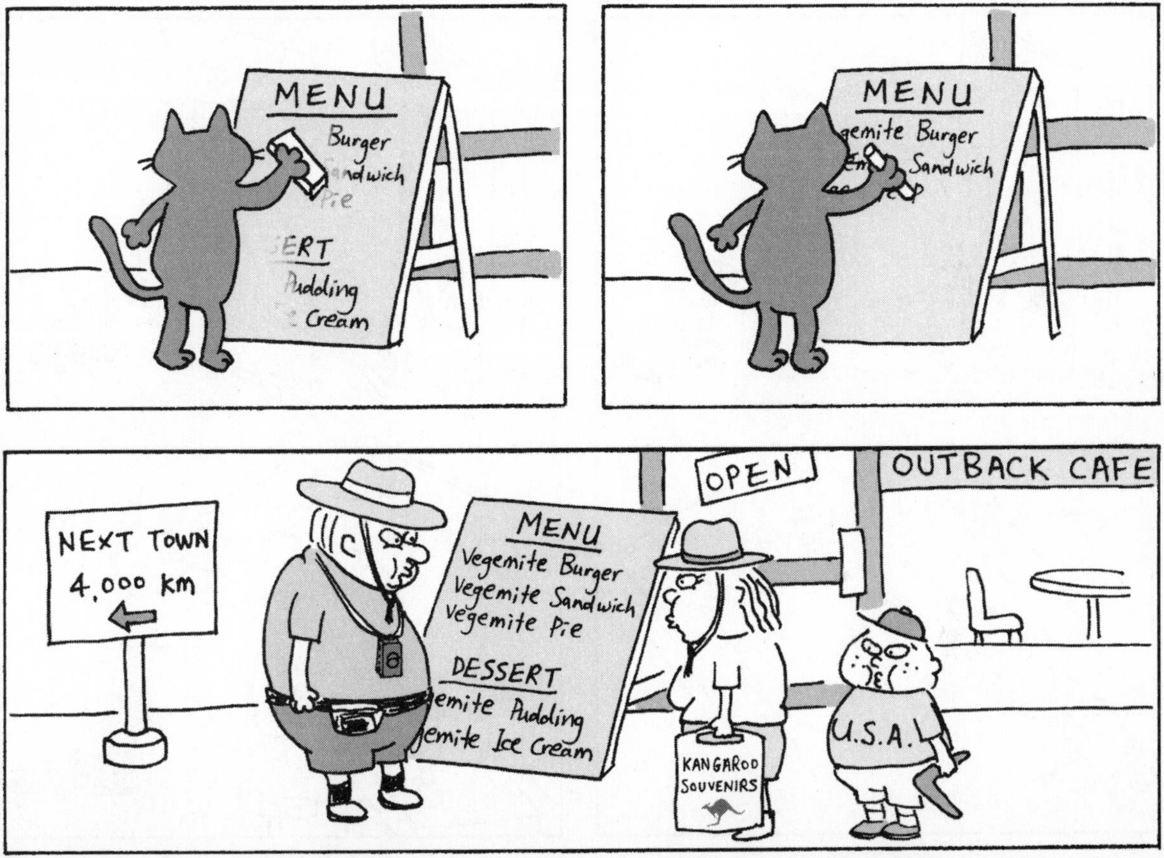

MENU
Burger
Pie
Pudding
Cream
MENU
Burger
Sandwich
NEXT TOWN
4,000 km
OPEN
OUTBACK CAFE
MENU
Vegemite Burger
Vegemite Sandwich
Vegemite Pie
DESSERT
Pudding
Ice Cream
KANGAROO SOUVENIRS
U.S.A.

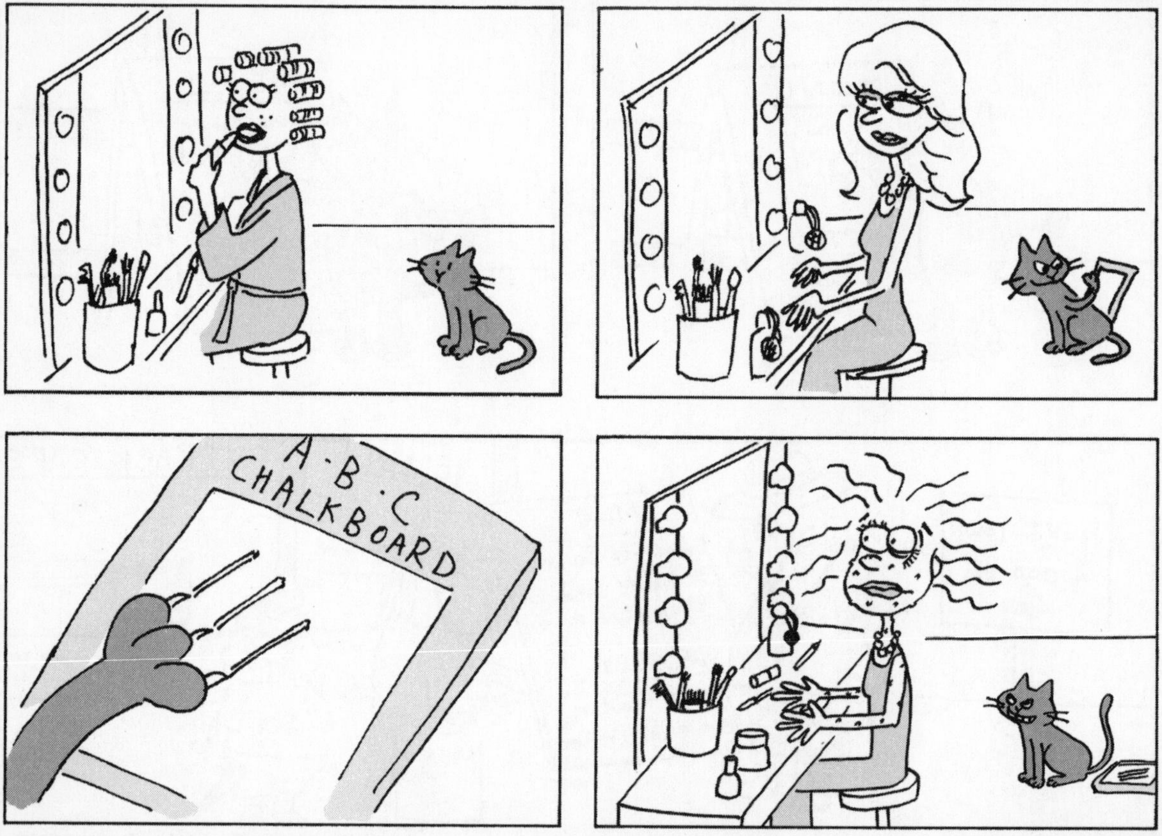
A · B · C
CHALKBOARD

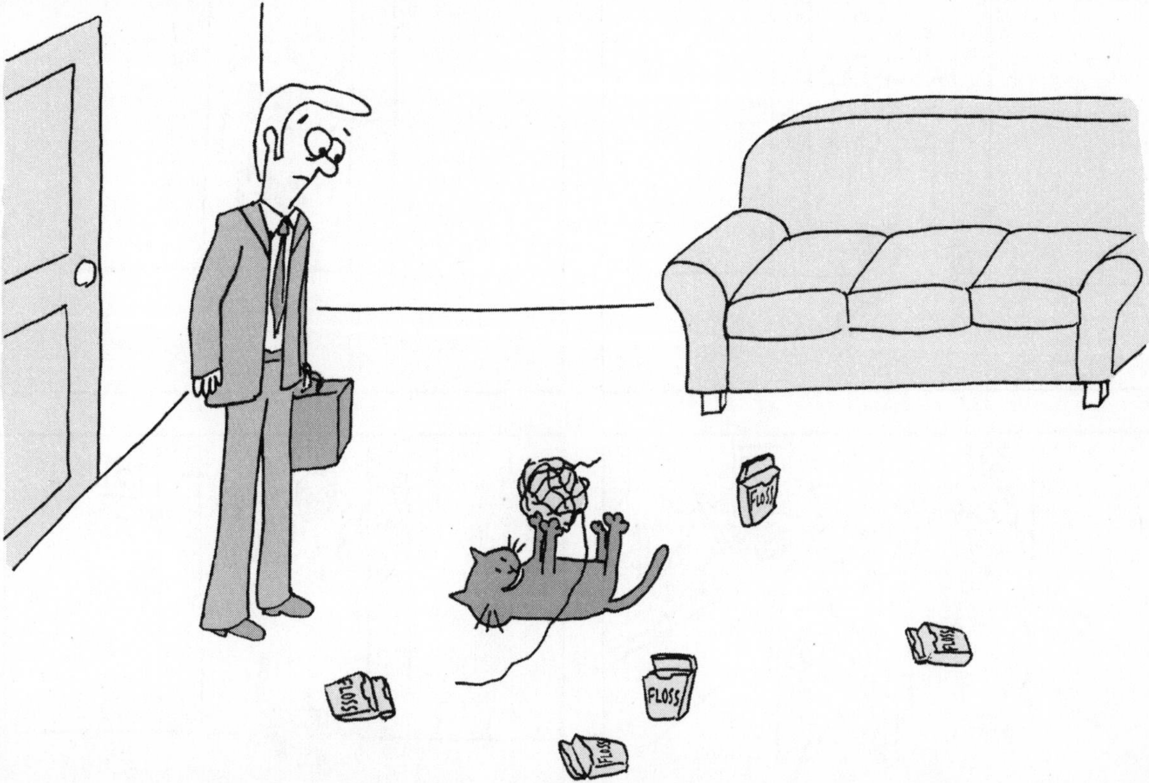
FLOSS
FLOSS
FLOSS
FLOSS
FLOSS

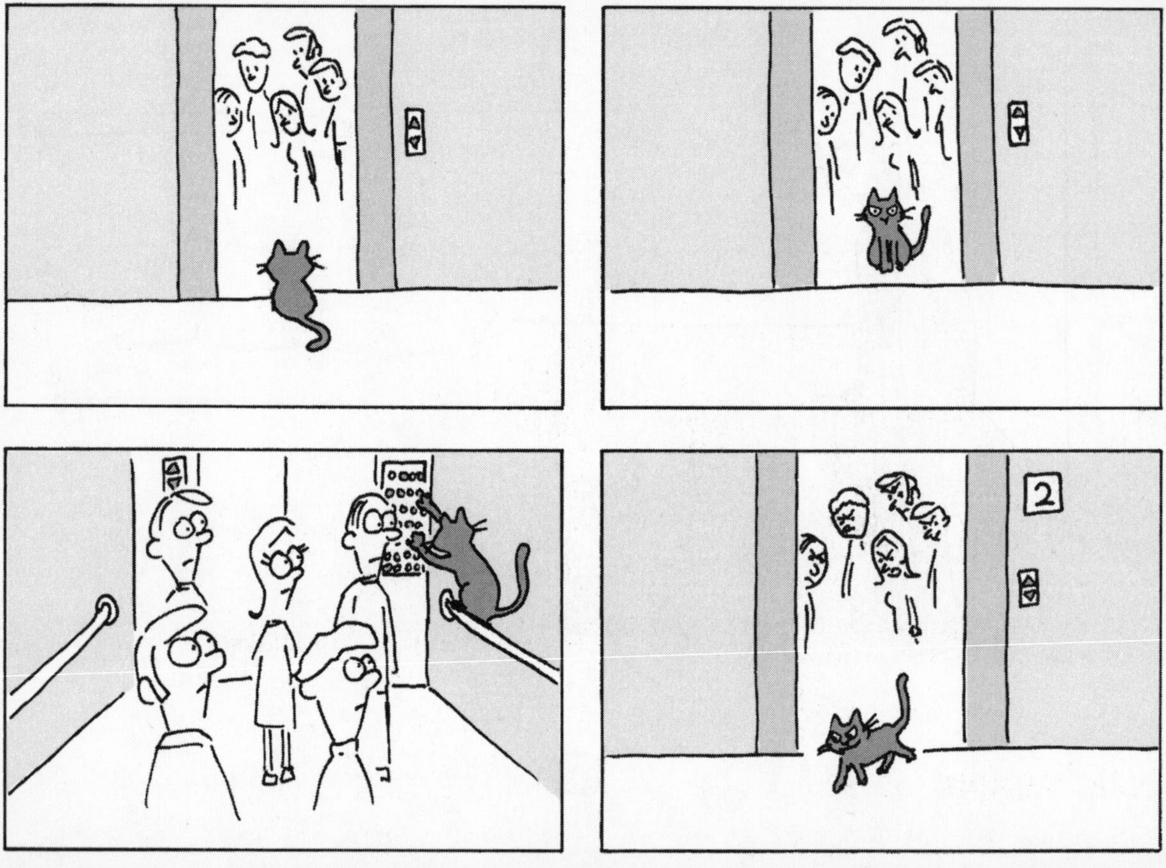
2

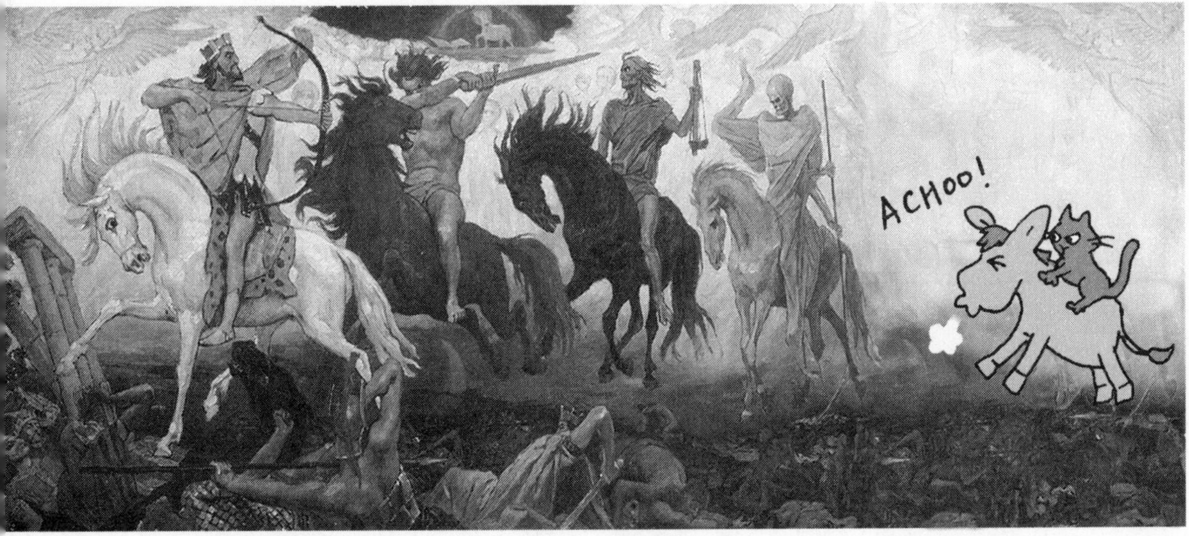
ACHOO!

THE FIVE HORSEMEN OF THE APOCALYPSE:
WAR, FAMINE, PESTILENCE, DEATH... AND VERY BAD ALLERGIES.

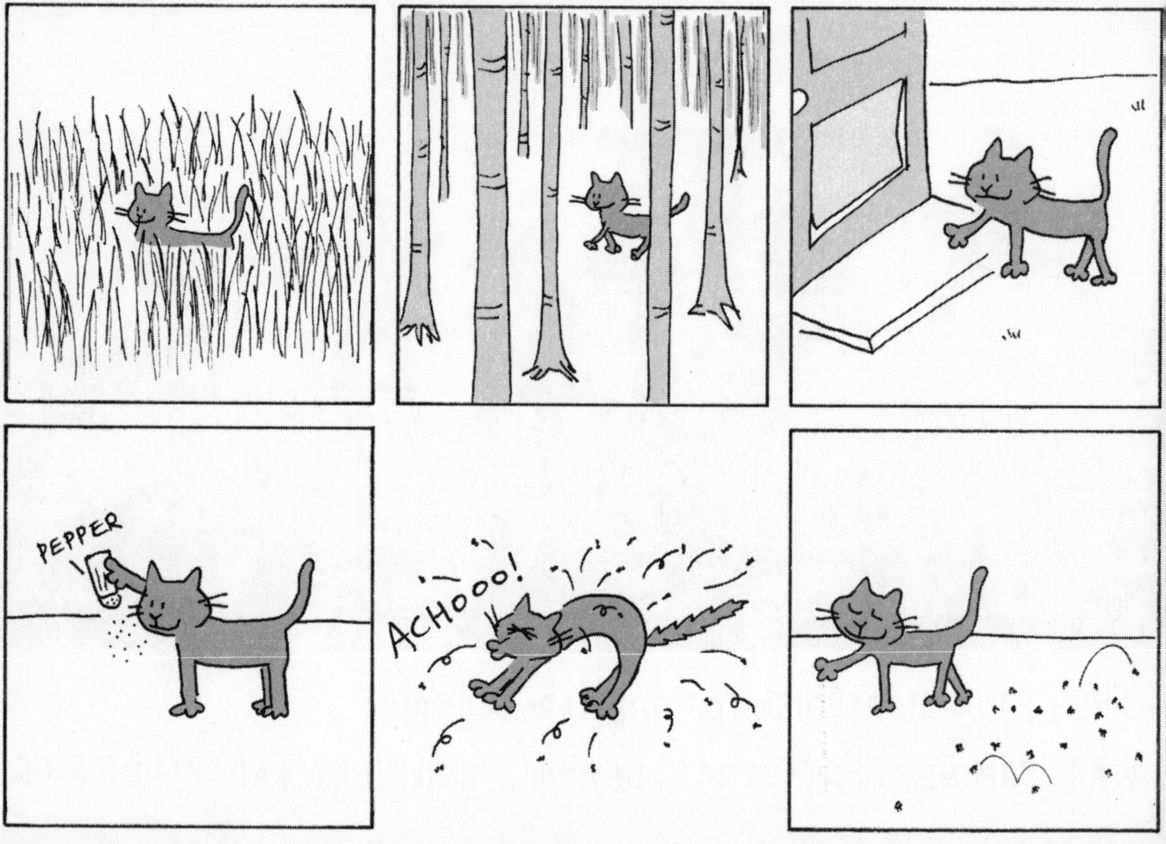
PEPPER
ACHOOO!

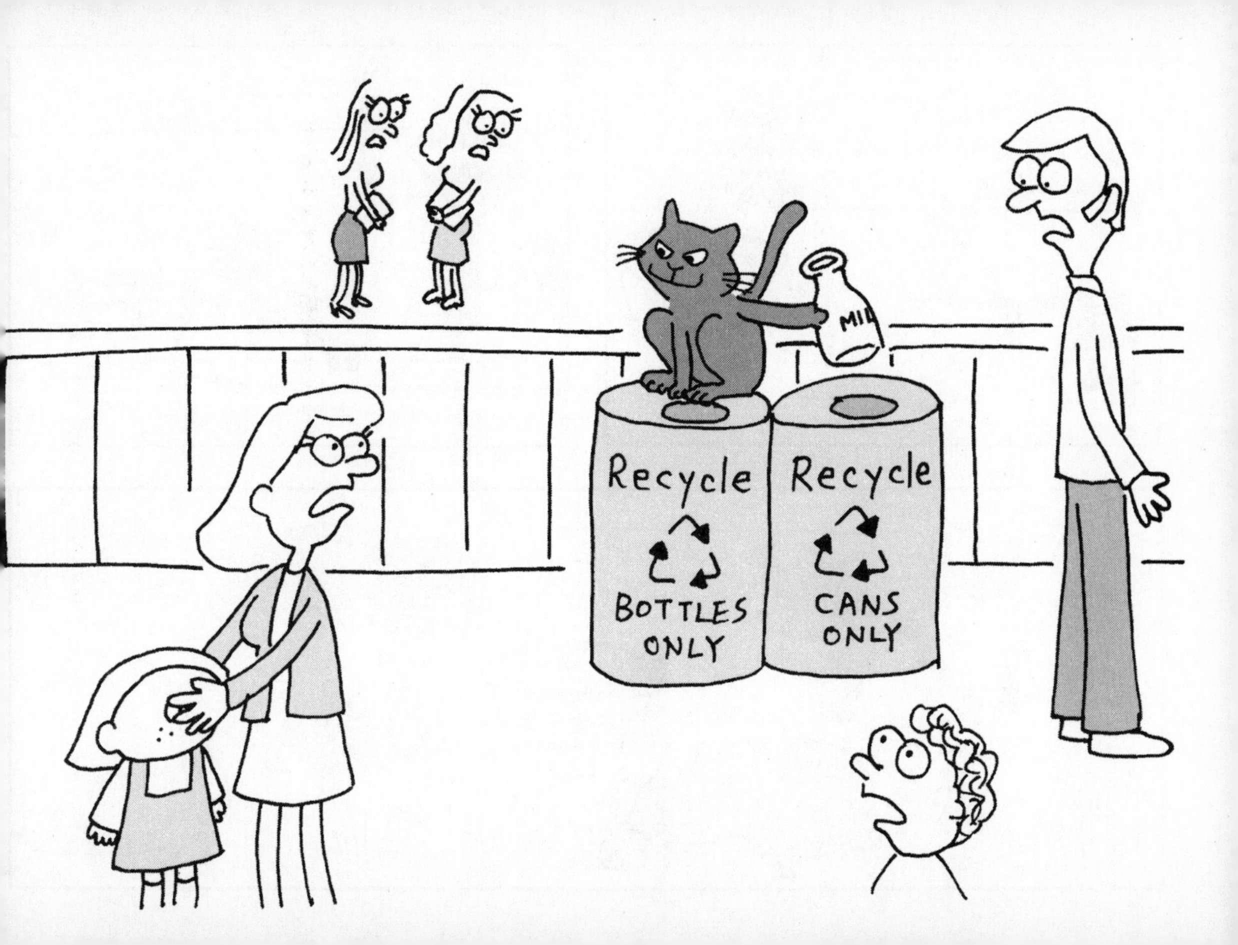
MIL
Recycle
BOTTLES ONLY
Recycle
CANS ONLY

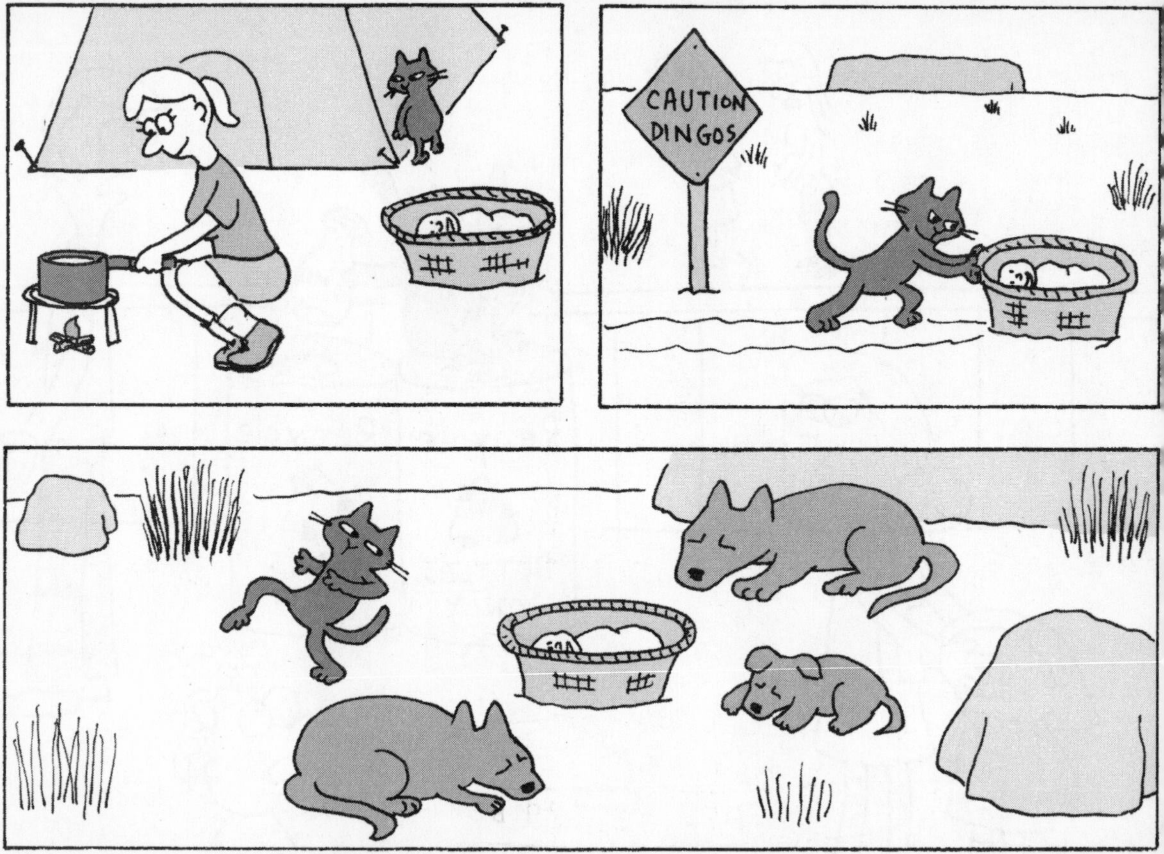
CAUTION
DINGOS

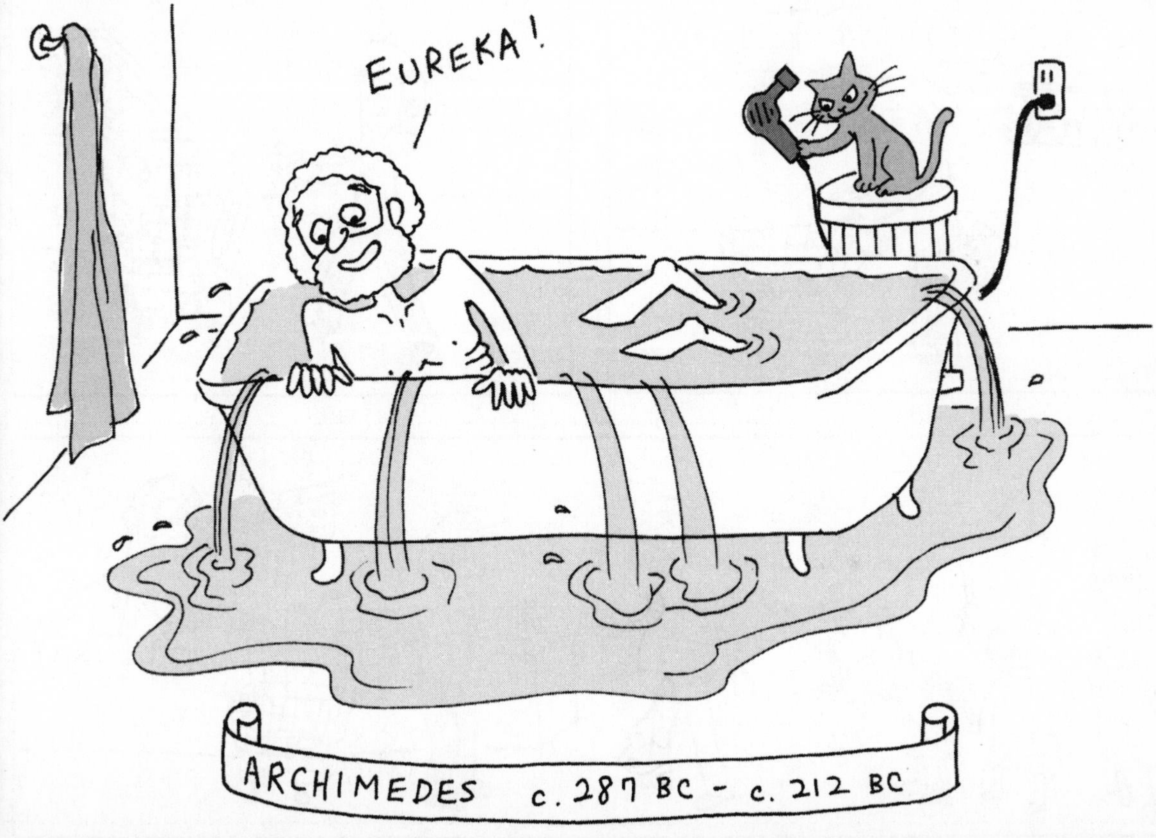
EUREKA!
ARCHIMEDES c. 287 BC - c. 212 BC

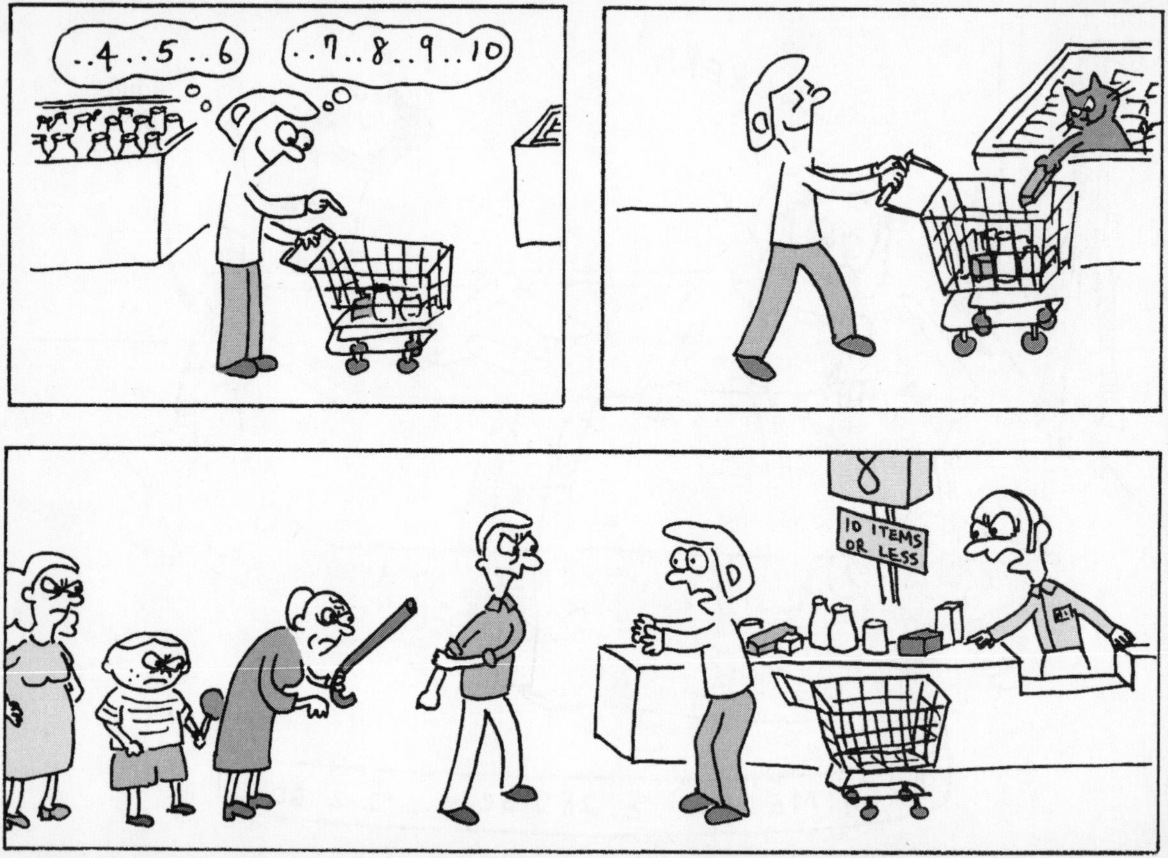
..4...5...6
..7..8...9...10
8
10 ITEMS OR LESS

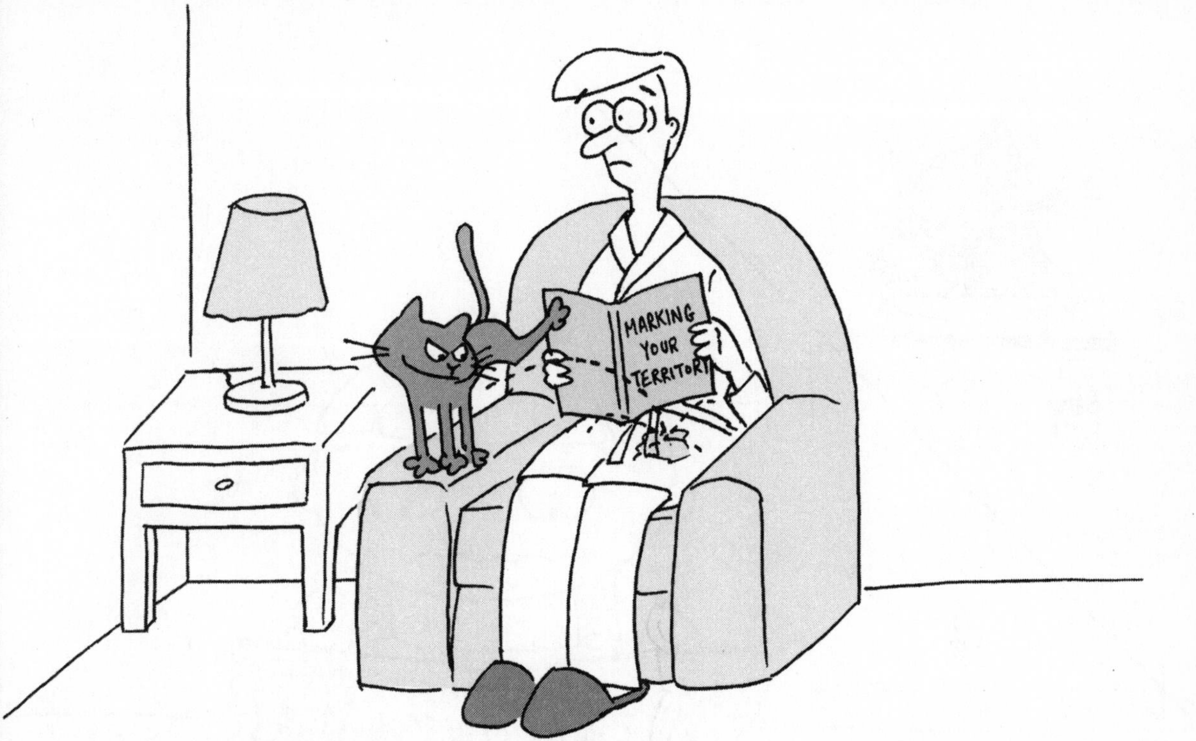
MARKING
YOUR
TERRITORY

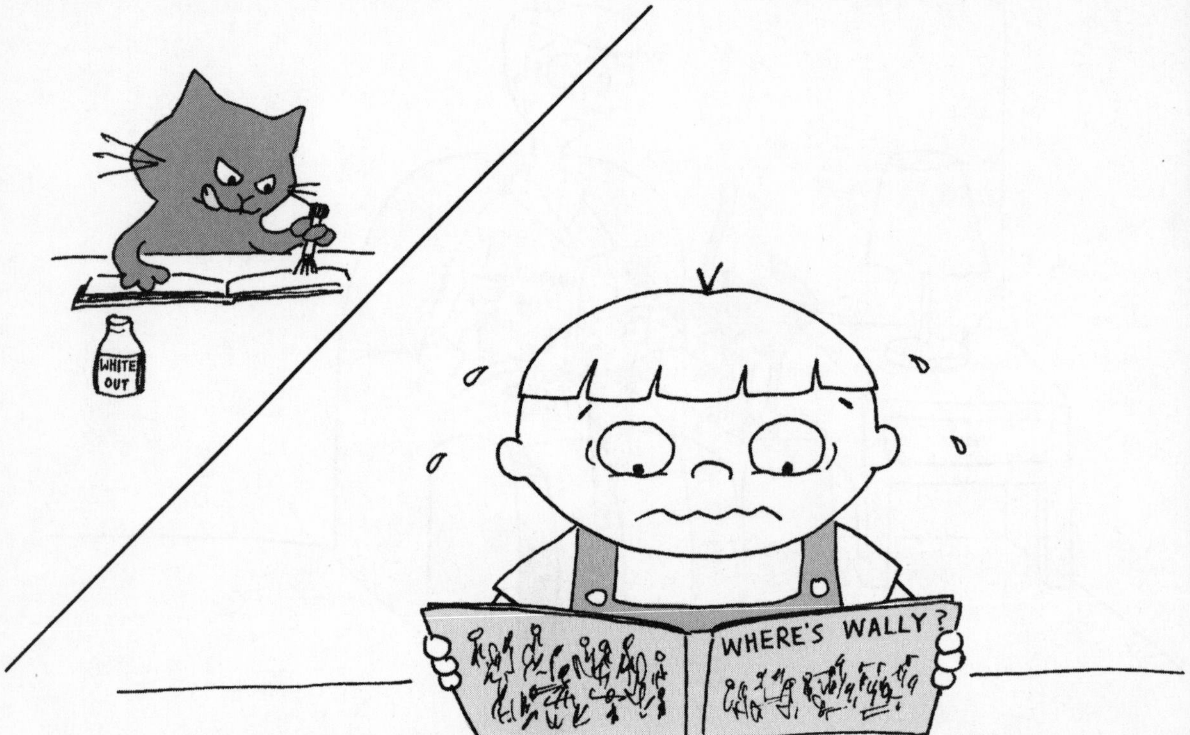
WHITE OUT
WHERE'S WALLY?

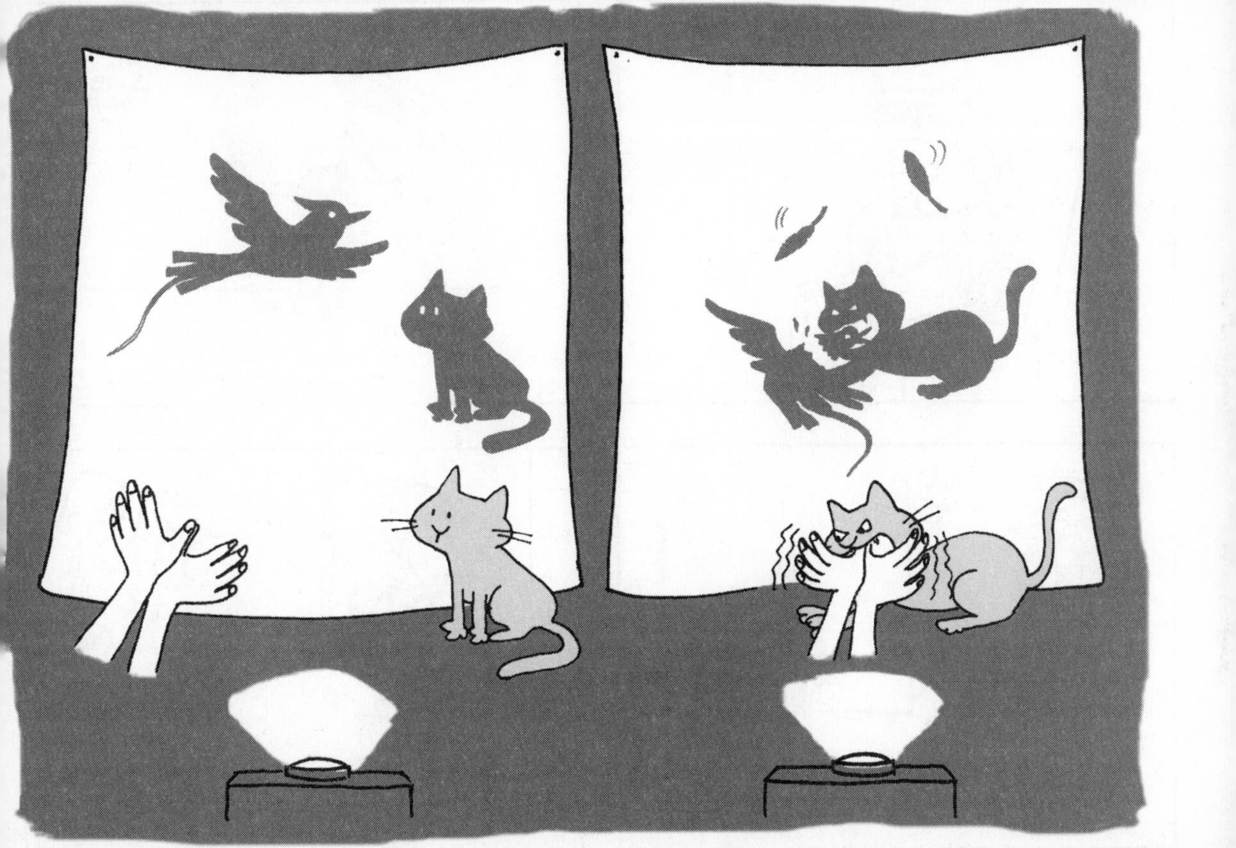

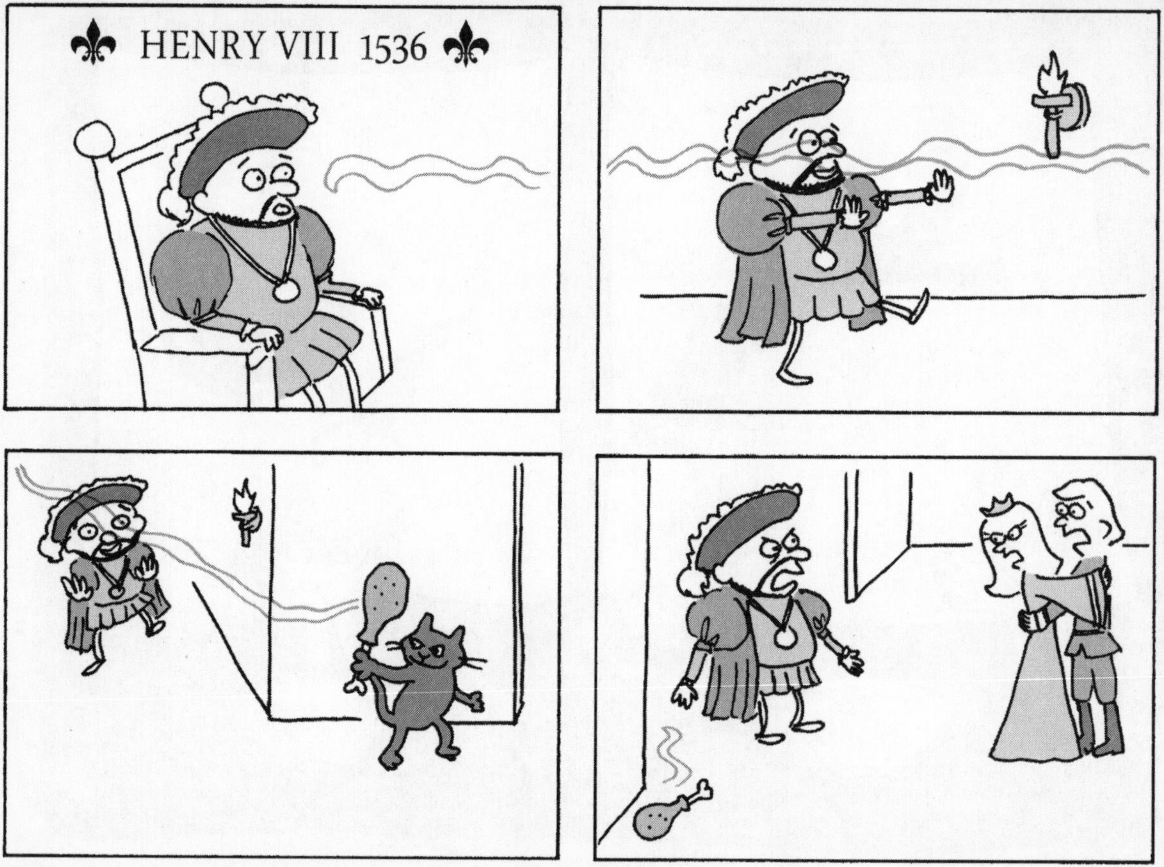
HENRY VIII 1536

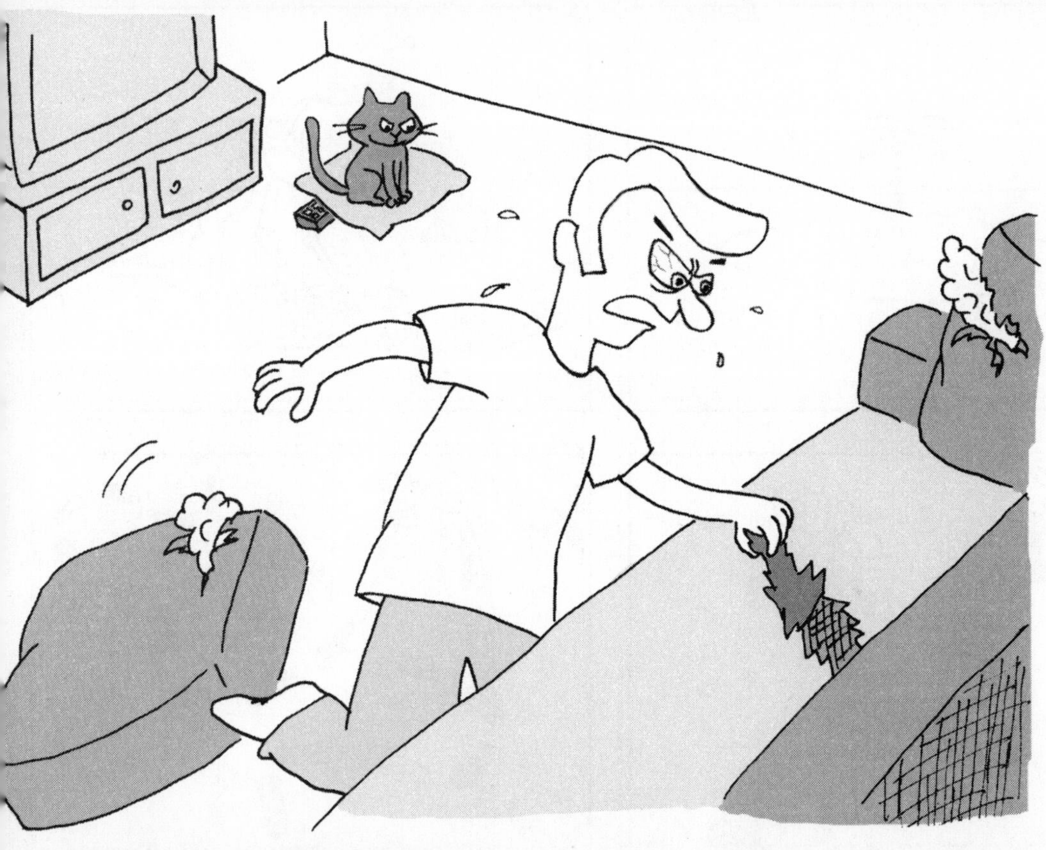

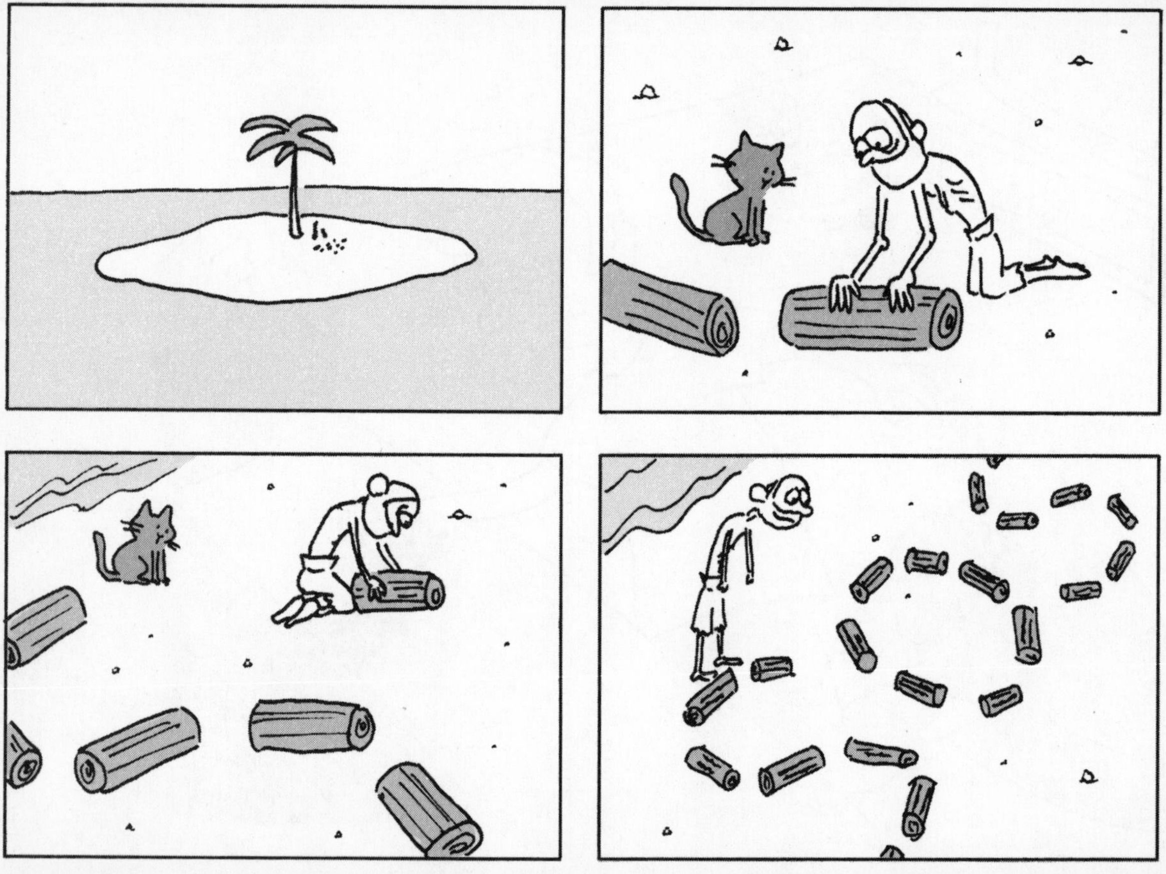

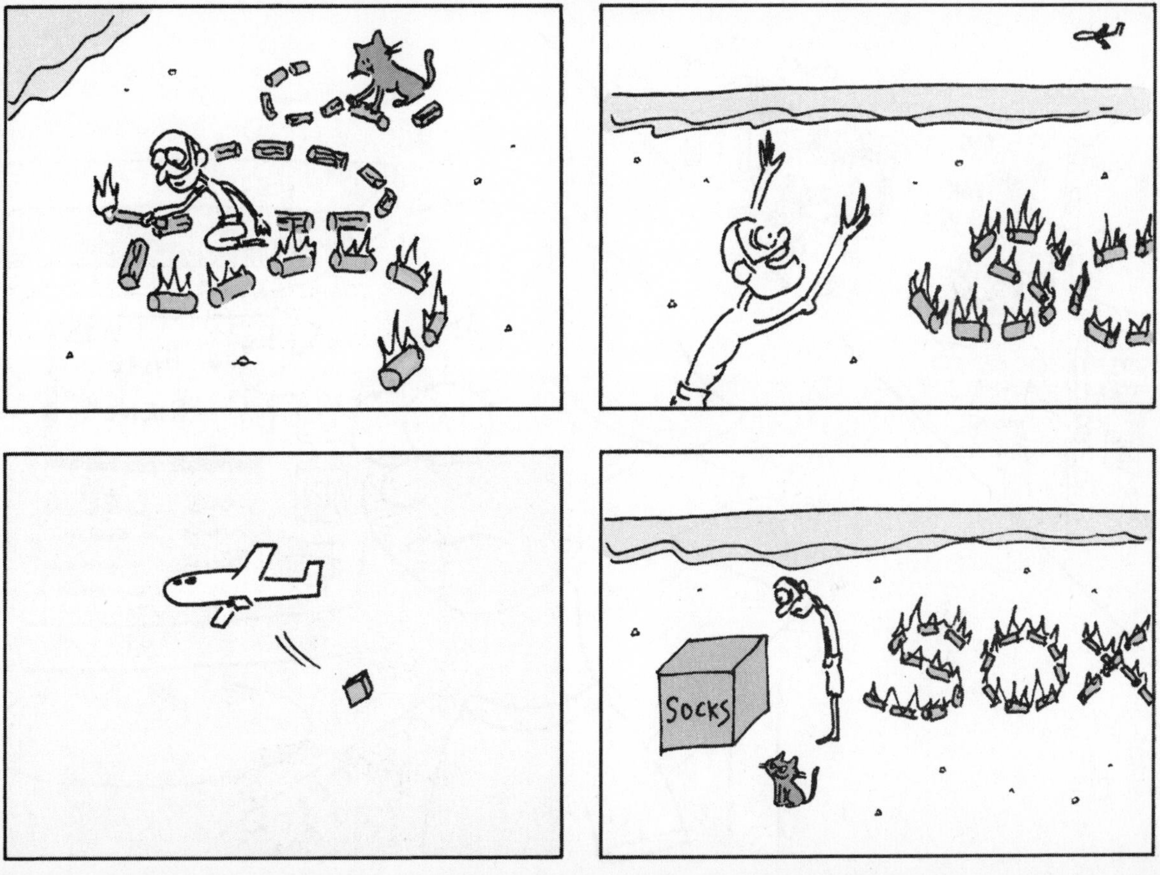
SOCKS
SOX

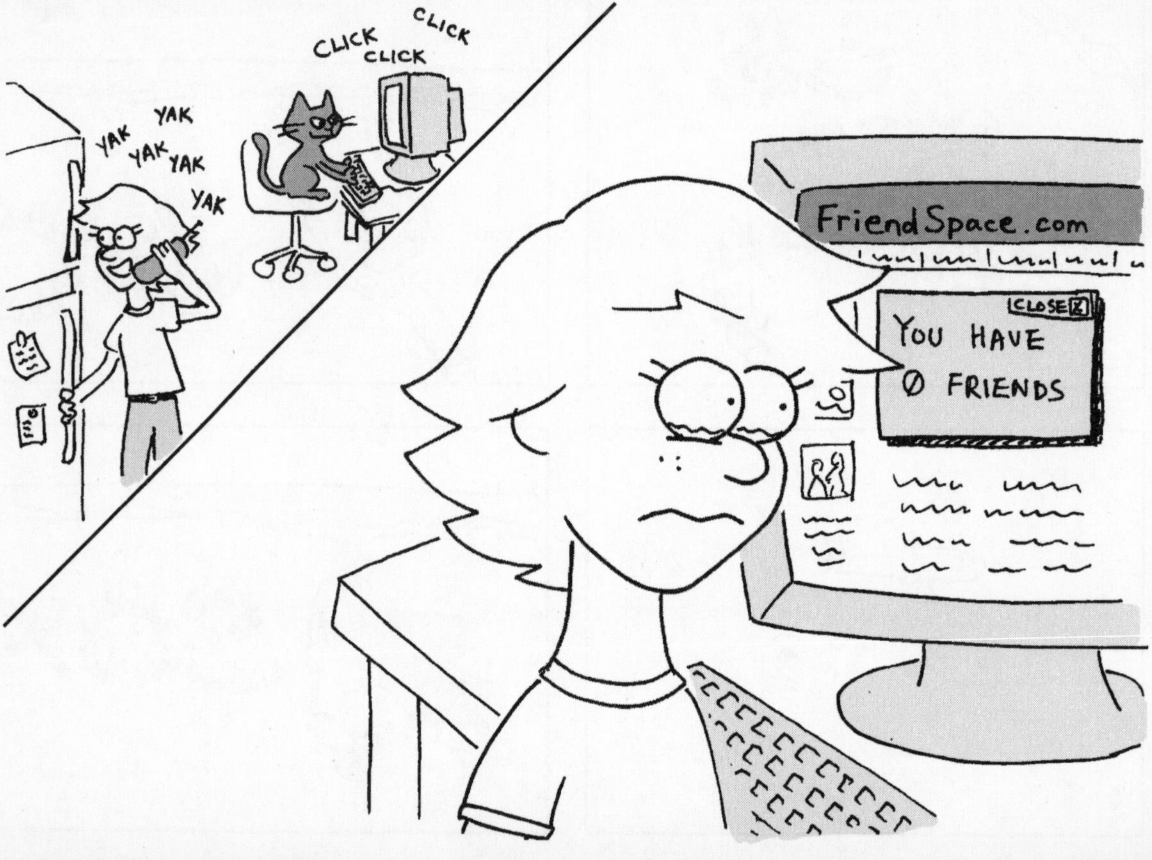
YAK
YAK
YAK
YAK
YAK
CLICK
CLICK
CLICK
FriendSpace.com
CLOSE X
YOU HAVE
Ø FRIENDS

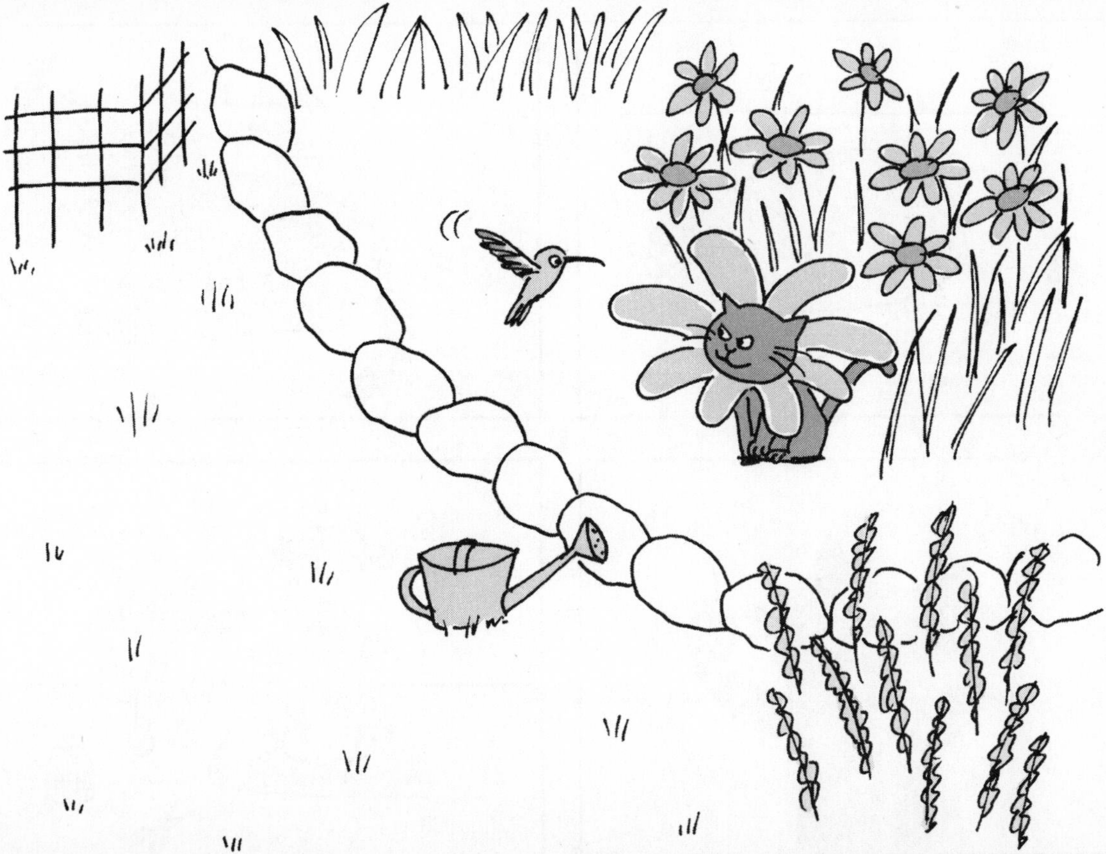

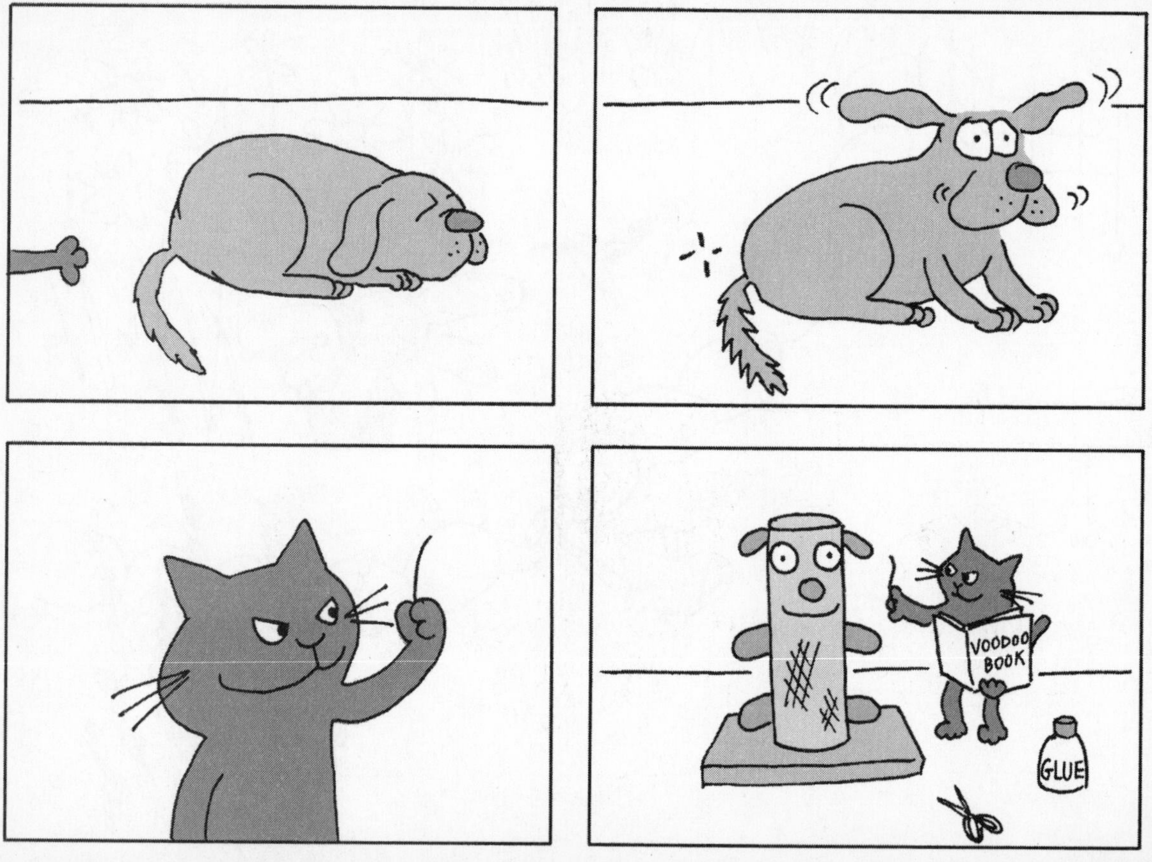
VOODOO BOOK
GLUE

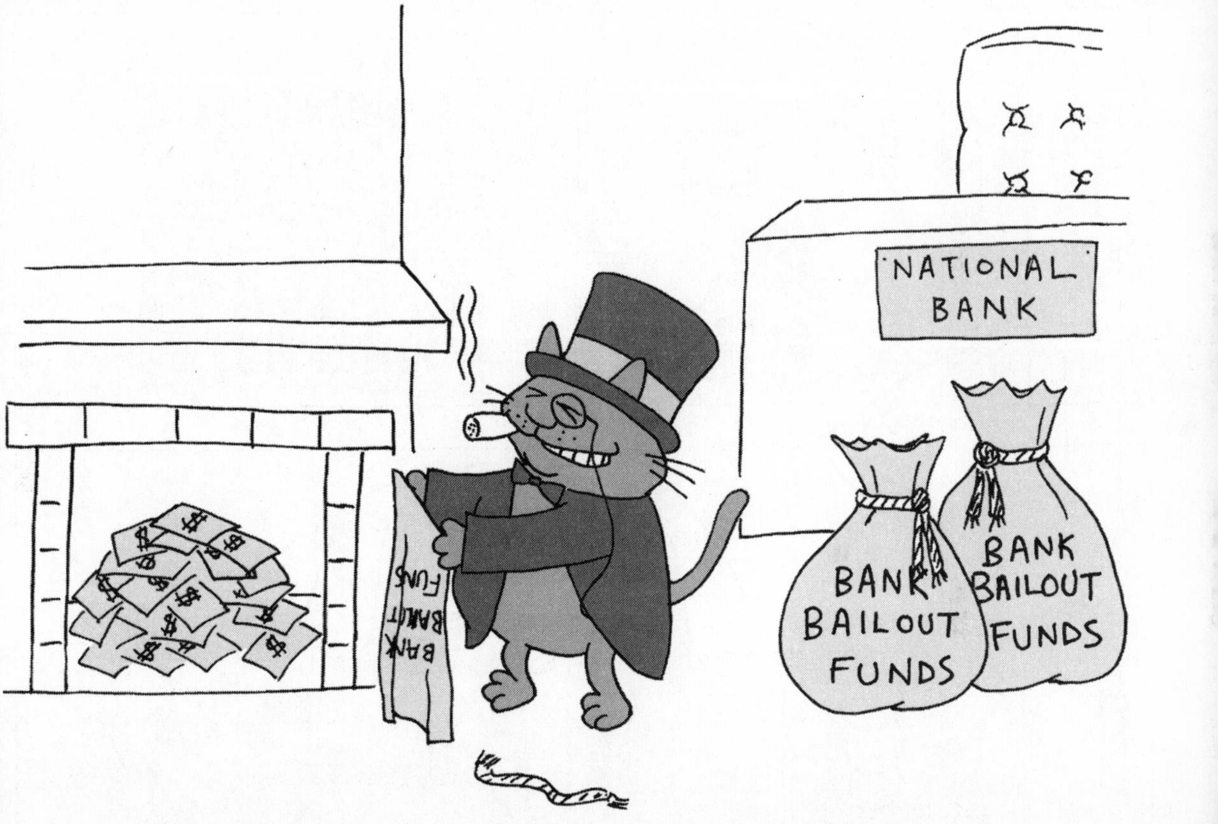
NATIONAL BANK
BANK BAILOUT FUNDS
BANK BAILOUT FUNDS

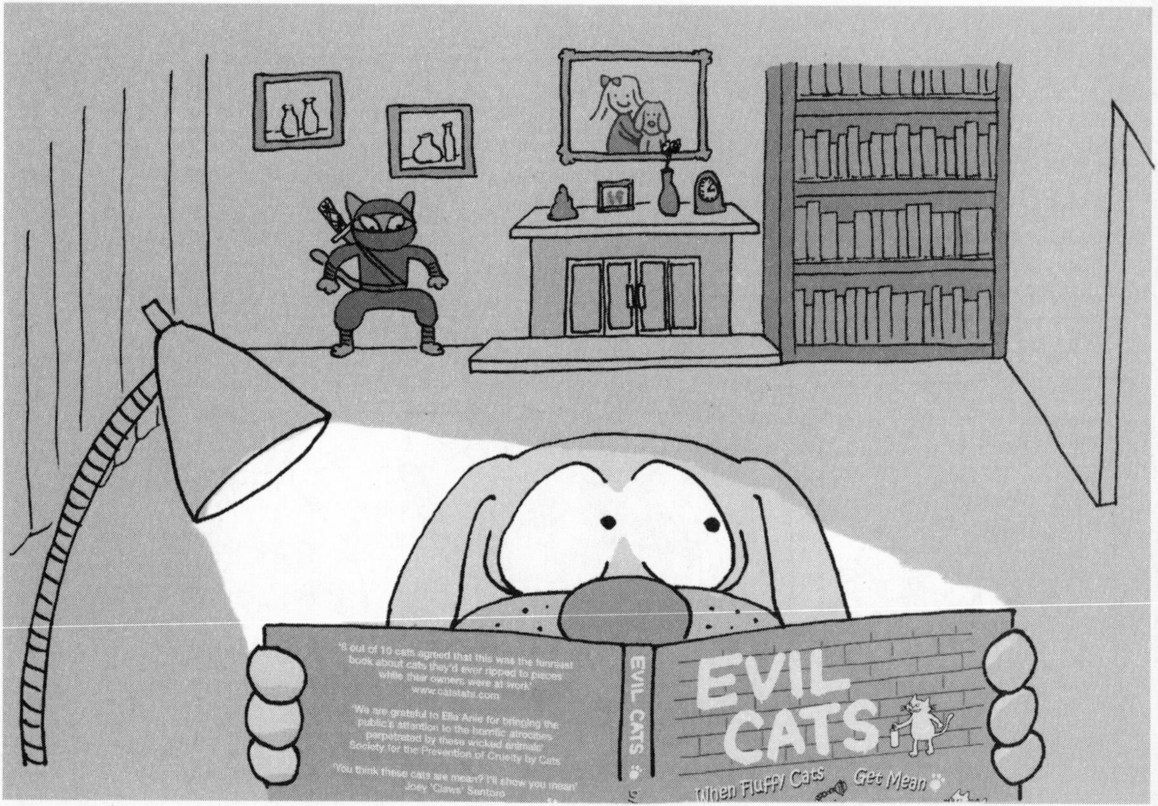
'8 out of 10 cats agreed that this was the funniest book about cats they'd ever ripped to pieces while their owners were at work'
www.catstats.com
'We are grateful to Ella Anie for bringing the public's attention to the horrific atrocities perpetrated by these wicked animals'
Society for the Prevention of Cruelty by Cats
'You think these cats are mean? I'll show you mean'
Joey 'Claws' Santoro
EVIL CATS
EVIL CATS
When Fluffy Cats Get Mean

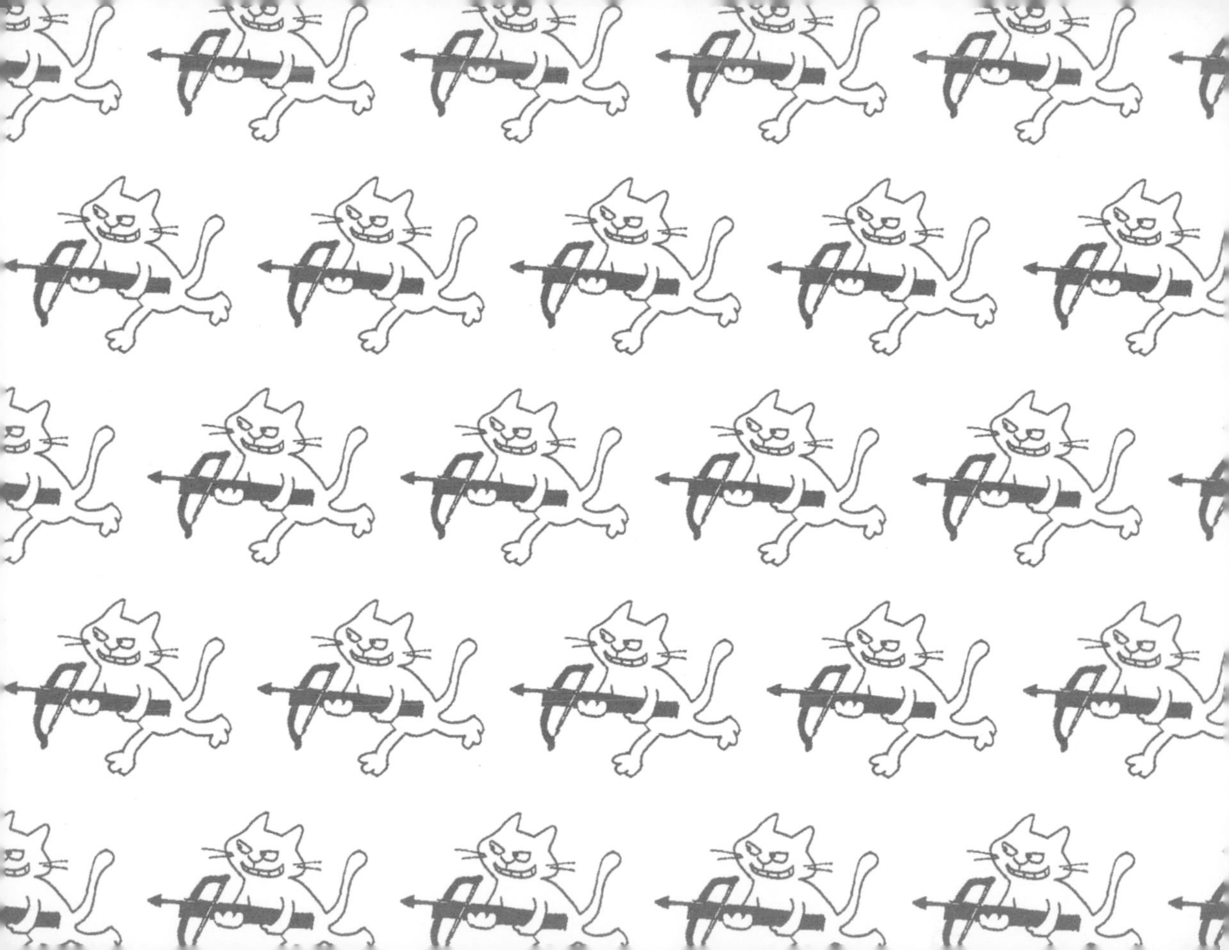